ON THE MARGINS
the Educational Experience of 'Problem' Pupils

ON THE MARGINS
the Educational Experience of 'Problem' Pupils

Edited by
Mel Lloyd-Smith and John Dwyfor Davies

Trentham Books

First published in 1995 by Trentham Books Limited

Trentham Books Limited
Westview House
734 London Road
Oakhill
Stoke-on-Trent
Staffordshire
England ST4 5NP

British Cataloguing in Publication Data
A catalogue record for this book is available from the British Library
ISBN: 1 85856 049 7

Designed and typeset by Trentham Print Design Ltd., Chester and printed in Great Britain by Shafron Bemrose (Printers) Limited, Chester

Contents

Chapter 1
**Introduction: Issues in the Educational Careers of
'Problem' Pupils**
Mel Lloyd-Smith and John Dwyfor Davies   1

Chapter 2
**Schools by Scoundrels: the Views of 'Disruptive' Pupils in
Mainstream Schools in England and the United States**
Philip Garner   17

Chapter 3
Out of the Spotlight: Girls' Experience of Disruption
Jo Crozier and Judith Anstiss   31

Chapter 4
Perceptions of Exclusion by Pupils with Special Needs
Susan de Pear   49

Chapter 5
**A 'Dunce's Place': pupils' perceptions of the role of a
special unit**
Anne Sinclair Taylor   67

Chapter 6
**When Segregation Works: Pupils' Experience of Residential
Special Provision**
Paul W. Cooper   87

Chapter 7
**Former Pupils' Reflections on Residential
Special Provision**
Tanya Howe   111

Chapter 8
**Exploring Pupils' Perceptions of their Experience in
Secure Accommodation**
Philip Colville Craig   133

Chapter 9
Gaining Access to Pupil Perspectives
Robert G. Burgess   151

Chapter 10
From Data to Action
Richard Davis   167

Notes on the Contrubutors   181

Index of Subjects   183

Index of Names   185

Chapter 1

Introduction: Issues in the Educational Careers of 'Problem' Pupils

Mel Lloyd-Smith and John Dwyfor Davies

Introduction

A significant number of children receive their education outside main-stream provision as a result of having been defined as 'problems' within the school system. They have, for varying lengths of time and to different degrees, been segregated from their peers as a consequence of their perceived disruptiveness: their truancy, bullying, aggression, delinquency or their inability to conform to the behavioural demands of their schools. The precise number is difficult to ascertain. For those who are referred to alternative provision through formal assessment and placement systems, figures do exist but where less formal or temporary measures are invoked, reliable statistics are rare. For example, while most authorities (including the DFE and Ofsted) agree that exclusion from school is currently increasing, there is no means of knowing the real extent at the present time (Blyth and Milner, 1993, Lloyd-Smith, 1993).

1

With regard to children who are formally referred to special schools on the grounds of emotional and behavioural difficulties, clearer indications are available and again, there is evidence of an increasing trend. Swann (1985 and 1988) has shown that despite the rhetoric of integration and the political impetus offered to this by the 1981 Education Act, the percentage of pupils educated in segregated provision is steadily increasing. Specifically, Swann suggests that the increase in segregated placements for pupils with emotional and behavioural difficulties and for those with moderate learning difficulties, is significantly greater than that for children with sensory disabilities.

Official statistics inevitably disguise the real extent of the population of pupils whose education in the mainstream has been interrupted as a result of behavioural problems, since they do not take account of the many referred to special units for disruptive pupils. This is further complicated as a result of the lack of stable statistics regarding pupils placed in residential care or secure provision.

The substantial literature on behavioural problems is predominantly concerned with methods of managing behaviour in the classroom or strategies for dealing with groups of 'problem' pupils in mainstream settings, special units or special schools. Understandably there have been strenuous efforts to provide teachers with techniques for alleviating one of the most insidious and persistent sources of stress in their professional role. This body of literature, however, does have its *lacunae*, one of which is insight into the felt experience of these pupils and their assessment of the effectiveness of the strategies adopted. Focus on the mechanics of managing behaviour can too readily distract attention from the central players — the pupils experiencing displacement from the mainstream, which is likely to be viewed with relief by those charged with providing an effective educational environment for the majority. This was recognised by the National Curriculum Council in its influential document on meeting the curriculum needs of all children:

> For pupils with emotional/behavioural problems, there are dangers in over-emphasis on 'managing' the behaviour without attempts to understand the child's feelings (NCC, 1989, p35).

'Problem' Pupils

This volume is concerned with the perceptions of that part of the school population whose behaviour has proved problematic to teachers and administrators and who consequently experienced a disrupted or non-normal educational career. There is not an adequate term to encompass these young people. In the vernacular they are 'problem' pupils though, as will be seen, their characteristics and circumstances are so diverse that any global label or theory is unlikely to be helpful in understanding their needs. Those featured in this book include boys and girls in mainstream schools who have been identified as disruptive or disaffected and in some instances excluded. Other cases are of pupils who have been formally assessed and categorised as having emotional and behavioural difficulties (EBD) and referred to a special unit or a day or residential special school. Another group represented is that of young people placed in a secure unit.

Prior to the introduction of the 1993 Education Act, pupils could be excluded from mainstream education indefinitely or permanently, under the provisions of the 1986 Education (No 2) Act. The new legislation however, abolishes the category of 'indefinite' exclusion and places a limit for which a pupil can be temporarily excluded, of up to 15 school days in any one term. DfE Circular 11/94 requires that for pupils permanently excluded, the local education authority retains responsibility for providing for their education in ways 'otherwise than at school' once it has upheld the school's decision (DfE, 1994a).

Despite the rhetoric of official documents such as Circular 11/94, seeking to minimise the number of pupils permanently excluded, it remains true that a significant and growing number continue to receive education in alternative settings. The Circular acknowledges that about 8,100 children in England and Wales were receiving education otherwise than in school on a census day in January 1993. Of these, 'a substantial proportion....had been excluded from school'. In addition to these, there is an unknown number of pupils who fall through the net and, sometimes for long periods, receive no education as a result of what Stirling (1992) refers to as 'unofficial' exclusion.

A substantial number of pupils find their way into residential special schools through the statutory processes of assessment and statementing. Of the 12,002 pupils attending the 215 residential special schools in England and Wales in 1994 (Saunders, 1994), the majority are placed on grounds of behaviour and/or behavioural difficulties. Wedell (1994) highlights the findings of Goacher et al., (1988) which present evidence that whilst the majority of the local education authorities are now educating more pupils with special educational needs in mainstream schools, in line with their policy statements for inclusive education, the one exception is the group of pupils with emotional and behavioural difficulties. The precise percentage is difficult to ascertain for reasons referred to earlier. There is considerable evidence that despite recent attempts to reverse the trend for segregated educational provision, local authorities continue to refer pupils to residential schools and units on the grounds of emotional and behavioural difficulties. It was noted earlier that such provision has continued to increase (Swann, 1988, Cole, 1989, Berridge, 1990). It is interesting to note that this seeming escalation continues despite a similar expansion in the lobby for inclusive education. At the same time, Social Services and many Local Education Authorities for both financial and policy reasons, are inclined to seek alternatives to the costly residential provision traditionally adopted (Scherer, 1990). Bennathan (1992) draws attention to the fact that one London borough prohibited its educational psychologists from recommending residential placement within the statement for pupils with special educational needs.

Barton and Tomlinson (1981) suggest that the increase in the identification and placement of pupils on the grounds of emotional and behavioural difficulty has less to do with a growth in the prevalence of emotional disturbance and more with professional extension of that definition. Howe (1993) argues that with reference to 'emotional and behavioural difficulty', it is particularly easy so to do, due to the lack of a precise, standardised procedure for measuring the degree of disturbance in those so described.

A small, but significant number of young people receive their education within secure accommodation as a result of extreme behaviour that warrants their exclusion from mainstream provision and, indeed, from liberty in general. In 1994, this amounted to approximately 300 young people (Craig, 1994). Section 25 of the Children Act 1989 stresses the need for care in ensuring the 'continuity of education' for all pupils placed in secure accommodation. It also describes the statutory framework governing the placement of these young people and stresses that this should be a 'last resort'. This is in line with the views of a number of commentators on this area of statutory provision. Millham et al. (1978), for example, voiced the view that:

> we must .... ensure that (secure provision) is used effectively for those children who need it. These are highly disturbed or neurotic absconders who will not settle in the best open care situations and a number of young people who are clearly a danger to the public (p.191).

Many others however, have for long expressed serious concern that secure provision has not always been decided upon with the care that the Children Act now requires. Cawson and Martell (1979), Children's Legal Centre (1982), Howard League for Penal Reform (1977), Millham et al (1978), Hoghughi (1978) and Harris and Timms (1993) have sounded alarms regarding the indiscriminate ways in which some young people were so placed, highlighting the long recognised need for statutory guidance to help ensure that this provision is available only for that minority who can not be educated within a more open context.

Issues of Policy and Legislation

Despite the lack of consensus about terminology and so-called causes for this range of problematic behaviour, there has been a running debate about of methods for dealing with 'problem' pupils. Approaches have changed in line with prevailing social attitudes, fluctuating from segregation to inclusion, from punishment to reform or from institutional conditioning to rehabilitation in the community. The issue has seldom been far from the front line of public and professional debate yet our understanding of the young people involved remains rudimentary as does our ability to provide effective strategies for dealing with the problems they pose. Partly because of the interest of the media and the periodic dissection of *causes celebres*, the image presented of these children tends to be a distorted one, they have often become mythologised, demonised and pathologised. The result of this is that generalised assumptions are made about their needs and insufficient account taken of individual experience and circumstances. Epidemiological studies of delinquency or truancy by their nature reveal little of the human beings to whom they relate; similarly reviews of provision or policy frequently indicate only the most shadowy impression of their real subjects.

The stimulus for this book comes from renewed concern about the increasing marginalisation of these young people at a time when resources for special provision are under threat and there is government encouragement to 'condemn a little more and understand a little less' (a phrase used in this context by Prime Minister John Major in a party political broadcast on 20.1.93). Deviant or disaffected pupils have become particularly vulnerable in the education market created in the UK in the past decade. There are signs that the covert processes which led to what Booth (1987) referred to as the 'devaluation' of pupils are now becoming overt under the new policies ostensibly designed to maximise choice and raise standards.

Amongst other measures, the 1988 Education Reform Act institutionalised competition between neighbouring schools as a means of raising standards. In the initial stages, the new legislation made scant reference to children with special needs of any kind; the emphasis was on providing incentives for those who would be most likely to succeed and thus enhance a school's marketability and power to attract funding. School governing bodies were given strong encouragement to review their policies relating to pupils who are the most difficult to teach and concentrate on those who can bring most credit to a school.

The introduction of these market mechanisms into state education was accompanied by widespread predictions that some pupils would be increasingly marginalised, that the interests and rights of some children with special educational needs and behavioural problems would not be fairly or adequately met. Research into the consequences of recent educational reform is now beginning to show that these predictions were wellfounded. The Centre for Studies on Inclusive Education has recently demonstrated that the increased percentage of the school population now being referred to segregated special, schools is linked to the operation of market forces in the mainstream sector (Norwich, 1994). There is also evidence that the current escalation in school exclusion is connected to the use of this sanction as a means of regulating access to schools competing in the market place for the most 'rewarding' pupils (Stirling, 1992, Cohen and Hughes, 1993).

The concept of 'deservingness' emerges clearly from a major study of the UK education market. Gerwitz et al (1995) have analysed the way in which the concept of equity has been used in justifications for market-driven policies. They have identified two competing conceptions of equity: needs-based and desert-based and it is the latter which is powerfully embedded in government thinking and policy and which carries an implicit connotation of 'deservingness'. The motivated, conforming and industrious are deserving of the opportunities offered by the education system, while the poorly motivated and deviant are not. Gerwitz et al's empirical study of market policies in action bears this out showing that schools are increasingly oriented towards meeting the demands of white, middle class parents and that resources are being diverted from those with the most needs to those with the fewest.

The devolution of financial resources to schools under the Local Management of Schools (LMS), confronts the governors and senior managers of mainstream schools with particular dilemmas. The education of pupils with special educational needs generally, and those exhibiting behavioural difficulties in particular, brings with it considerable cost implications (Russell, 1990). For schools functioning within a fixed budget, serious consideration has to be given as to how best to apportion that money. These are the very pupils who are unlikely to reflect positively on the school's reputation and are, at the same time, expensive to educate. It thus becomes additionally difficult to justify to parents, increased spending on them in preference to resources for pupils who are less problematic and likely to achieve in a competitive climate. In addition to the requirement to be openly accountable for the way they distribute this devolved funding, school governors also have to operate within the fixed sum that they are allocated. With the demise of the support traditionally offered by local education authorities as a regular part of their services to schools, head teachers and governors are presently having to purchase these services. The implications of this rebound significantly on those pupils who are likely to make additional demands on that limited funding. Coopers and Lybrand (1988) noted that

> If schools had the responsibility to 'buy in' psychological, welfare or medical services, such resource decisions would need to be balanced against other demands for resources. This might encourage a tendency in schools to under-purchase such services and seek to make do with staff less professionally qualified, perhaps at the expense of the pupil(s) concerned (p.17).

Pupils exhibiting behaviour difficulties are amongst the most obvious of those likely to suffer directly in light of pressures on scarce resources — frequently resulting in their exclusion from the mainstream. The 'market economy' will thus tend to reduce the concerns of managers for the education of such pupils and will encourage them to see the responsibility as lying elsewhere. This tendency was revealed in recent research conducted by Ingrid Lunt and Jennifer Evans (1994):

> The reduction in centrally provided special needs support services, the documented increase in demand for statements, a trend towards more placements in special schools and the rise in numbers of pupils excluded from schools point to some of the effects of recent legislation on special educational needs (p.48).

In view of this, a concern about the marginalisation of those who attract the label of 'problem pupil' would seem to be justified and there is a strong case for saying that their entitlement, as well as their needs and their actual experience, should be monitored constantly.

Listening to pupils' perspectives.

The 1989 Children Act requires that young people are offered an opportunity to contribute to the process of decision-making regarding their future interests. In the field of education, the 1993 Education Act follows this precedent which is more fully articulated within the 1994 Code of Practice (DfE 1994b) and accompanying Circulars, which offer clarification as to how this should be negotiated, and therefore acknowledge, by implication, the importance of listening to the views of children and young people. It should be noted however, that the Code of Practice, merely proposes that:

> schools should .... make every effort to identify the ascertainable views and wishes of the child or young person about his or her current and future education (paras 2.34-2.38).

The subsequent suggestions, outlining what it views as 'good practice' are similarly presented cautiously and in line with the general guidance offered within the Code. This caution is perhaps not surprising since, as Ron Davie (1993) points out, the 1993 Education Act, (when in the form of a Bill), 'made no reference to the views of pupils at all'. In the same article, he highlights the fact that the Elton Committee Report (DES, 1989a) was tentative in its recommendations regarding the direct involvement of pupils' and that the HMI publication 'Education Observed: Curriculum Continuity at 11-plus' (DES, 1989b) regretted the lack of attention paid by governors to the opinions of pupils, despite the fact that 'the majority of pupils were thoughtful, informative and articulate.' Tisdall and Dawson (1994) suggest however, that as a consequence of recent legal requirements, professionals have become increasingly aware of the importance of listening to the perspective of the pupils about whom concern is being expressed. They draw attention however, to the findings of Wade and Moore (1993), that, as yet, it is the minority of professionals who practice consultation with pupils to ascertain their views so as to influence subsequent intervention. As noted above, the concept of consulting 'consumers' regarding the services they receive is relatively recent. Within the education sector, the idea of consulting pupils began to make an impression with the introduction of Records of Achievement which emphasise students' successes and encourage them to discuss their progress with teachers. Several authors have recognised the importance of drawing upon the perceptions of pupils in evaluating their educational experiences. Gersch (1990) suggests that pupils should be more actively involved in planning their educational experiences and states that 'more could be done generally to elicit pupils' views of their school' (p.118). Lane and Green (1990) believe that the introduction of open access to pupils' files will go some way towards redressing the power differential between pupils and their teachers. In their opinion, pupils 'often feel that their own contribution to decision-making is devalued or not heard at all' (p.253). Macbeath and Thomas (1992) have recently supported this view with reference to school evaluations, whilst Pimenoff (1993) has begun to explore the concept of pupil involvement in the appraisal of their teachers.

Such moves signal a significant ideological shift away from that which views pupils as passive recipients, towards one which seeks to promote pupils' rights to consultation as consumers of education. Keys and Fernandes (1993) recognise that whilst pupils may not always be accurate in their observations, their perceptions are fundamental to the effectiveness of schools, since it is these perceptions which inform attitudes towards school and play a large part in determining pupil behaviour. Whilst it is acknowledged that pupil consultation is generally uncommon, and even more so if the pupils have special educational needs (Wade and Moore, 1993) or are considered disruptive (Garner, 1992), there is evidence to suggest that within certain sectors of the education system, this may not be the case. Therapeutic communities are well documented in the way that they often engage pupils in the management of their lives. Pupil involvement in decision-making has long been a central feature of such establishments (Cole, 1986). Wade and Moore attempt to demonstrate that pupils with special educational needs can provide honest, valid and illuminating accounts of their experience and suggest that the 'learner's viewpoint is an essential ingredient in helping to develop teaching which is child-centred rather than simply didactic' (p.5).

Whilst the 1981 Education Act gave parents the right to be consulted in the process leading to a Statement of Special Educational Needs, the first mention of the pupils themselves engaging in this process appeared in the DES Circular 1/83, which stated that

> the feelings and perceptions of the child concerned should be taken into account, and the concept of partnership should, wherever possible, be extended to older children and young persons (DES, 1983: Section 6).

The advantages of involving pupils in decision-making and creating opportunities for students to assume greater responsibilities as they get older are further identified in the Elton Report (DES, 1989) in terms of their contributing towards the promotion of good behaviour in schools. It is worth noting however, that it was not until the Children Act, 1989 that the sampling of the views and feelings of pupils was given legislative support. Whilst the main focus of this legislation is on the involvement of children in the process of planning for their care, it also has considerable implications for school:

> The Children Act should assist us in getting schools and other institutions to listen to children and to give them a voice. This is no longer simply good practice, but is enshrined in legislation (Mayet: 1992: 3).

Despite the official encouragement to increase pupil consultation and involvement, in the Children Act, in the Code of Practice and elsewhere, and despite widespread support in the educational literature, its adoption in practice is not yet extensive. Wade and Moore (1993) suggest that some teachers regard consultation as unnecessarily time-consuming and dangerous in that it may upset traditional power-based pupil-teacher relationships.

There is an important role for empirical research in providing the means for children to reflect on their educational experience and provide insights for policy makers and practitioners into the adequacy and effectiveness of provision. The debate about policy and strategy needs to be informed by the perceptions of the pupils themselves and there is relatively little evidence of this type available at the present time. Some notable exceptions are Wade and Moore, 1992, (children with a range of special needs); Cooper, 1993, (children with EBD); Kelly, 1992, (children in a secure unit); and Lewis, 1995 (children with severe learning difficulties). The need for this perspective on the educational careers of 'problem' pupils could be said to be particularly acute, given the tendency for their marginalisation and devaluation in the education market. The quality and effectiveness of the measures we adopt to deal with them affect their long-term educational and personal welfare and the long-term costs to society through later intervention and support.

The problems of research in this field are not insignificant. The subjects are often resentful, defensive, alienated and in some cases, disturbed. Their educational careers have invariably involved individual and family stress and invitations to discuss them are not always welcomed. The contributors to this volume have wrestled with these sensitivities and with the methodological problems of capturing authentic accounts. The authors include academic researchers looking from the outside at issues of effective policy and practice and teachers on the inside exploring their own work situations and setting out to understand more fully their day to day interaction with pupils. They have collectively used a variety of methodological approaches in their attempts to enter the world of pupils on the margins and to provide insights which, without focused research, might remain inaccessible.

Philip Garner uses a case study methodology to examine the views of pupils regarded in two schools as disruptive, one in the UK and one in the USA. The comparative style of his study usefully places the immediate and local issue of disruptive behaviour into a broader perspective. Jo Crozier and Judith Anstiss find a way of penetrating the pupil subculture

11

to examine insiders' views of classroom disruption as enacted or experienced by girls in a comprehensive school. Susan de Pear's study of a group of excluded pupils makes use of a formal analytical framework both to structure the data collection and to describe the pupils' interpersonal needs.

A combination of interview and observation is employed by Anne Sinclair Taylor to uncover the contrasts between the 'official' perceptions of a form of integrated provision and the perceptions of the pupils experiencing it from day to day. Paul Cooper uses data collected in a variety of ways to build up a picture of the experience of residential schooling; the insights of these children on the furthest margins of state education are used to suggest how mainstream schools might become more effective in dealing with their 'problem' pupils. In a second chapter on the experience of a residential special school, Tanya Howe uses both a postal questionnaire and interviews to examine the recollections of some of her former pupils. She reveals how they viewed this phase of their lives as well as the effect it had on their subsequent development. Philip Craig also investigates the impact of the institution in which he works on the young people referred to it; he uses existing data from personal files in combination with interviews to illuminate their views on the effectiveness of a secure unit as punishment and rehabilitation.

Some of the contributors discuss in detail the ethical and practical issues they encountered in conducting their research. All of their accounts illustrate both the problems and opportunities offered by small-scale research and reveal the potential value of such studies for the institutions concerned and for a wider audience. In a specially commissioned chapter, Robert Burgess discusses the problems of researching the perceptions and experience of children and young people. He considers the conflicts and dilemmas inherent in the role of adult researcher in educational settings and offers guidance on the ethical and practical problems of achieving critical and reliable evidence of pupils' points of view. A further specially commissioned chapter by Richard Davis poses the question of what is required to turn the insights of research such as this into action to change and enhance practice in schools. He offers a perspective which is both reactive and preventive and which provides the basis of change for the benefit of all pupils, not only those to whom the label of 'problem' has been attached.

Bibliography

Barton , L. and Tomlinson, S. (Eds.) (1981) *Special education: Policy, Practice and Social Issues*, London, Harper and Row

Berridge, D. (1990) Residential schools for children with emotional and behavioural difficulties: new research project, *Young Minds Newsletter*, 6, 14.

Bennathan, M. (1992) The care and education of troubled children, *Young Minds*, 10, 1-7

Blythe E and Milner J (1993) Exclusion from school: a first step in exclusion from society? *Children and Society* 7(3) pp. 255-268

Booth T (1987) Introduction in Booth T and Coulby D (eds) *Producing and Reducing Disaffection*, Milton Keynes, Open University

Cawson P and Martell M (1979) *Children Referred to Closed Units*, DSS Research Report No. 5, London, HMSO

Children's Legal Centre (1982) *Locked Up in Care*, London, Children's Legal Centre.

Cohen, R. and Hughes, M. (1994) *School's Out: the Family Perspective on School Exclusion,* London, FSU/Barnardos

Cole, T. (1986) *Residential Special Education*, Milton Keynes, Open University Press

Cole, T. (1989) *Apart or a Part? Integration and the Growth of British Special Education*, Milton Keynes, Open University Press.

Cooper P (1993) *Effective Schools for Disaffected Students: Integration and Segregation,* London, Routledge

Coopers and Lybrand, (1988) *Local Management of Schools. A report prepared by Coopers and Lybrand for the DES*, London, DES

Craig, P. (1994) Exploring Pupils' Perceptions of Their Experience in Secure Accommodation, Unpublished MEd Dissertation, University of the West of England, Bristol.

Davie, R. (1993) Listen to the child: a time for change, *The Psychologist*, 6 (6) pp.252-257

Department of Education and Science, (1983) *The Assessment of Special Educational Needs: Joint Circular 1/83*, London, HMSO

Department of Education and Science (1989a) *Discipline in Schools, (The Elton committee Report,* London, HMSO

Department of Education and Science (1989b) *Education Observed: Curriculum Continuity at 11-plus*, London, HMSO

Department for Education (1994a) *Circular 11/94 The Education by LEAs of Children Otherwise than at School,* London, DfE

Department for Education (1994b) *Code of Practice on the Identification and Assessment of Special Educational Needs*, London, DfE

Garner, P. (1992) Involving disruptive students in school discipline structures, *Pastoral Care*, 10(3) pp.13-19

GB Parliament (1993), *Education Act 1993*, London, HMSO

Gersch, I. (1990) Pupils' views, in Scherer, M., Gersch, I and Fry, L. (eds.) *Meeting Disruptive Behaviour,* London, Macmillan

Gerwitz S, Ball S and Bowe R (1995) *Markets, Choice and Equity in Education,* Milton Keynes, Open University Press

Goacher, B. et al. (1988) *Policy and Provision for Special Educational Needs*, London, Cassell

Harris R and Timms N (1993) *Secure Accomodation in Child Care: Between Hospital and Prison or Thereabouts,* London, Routledge

Hoghughi M (1978) *Troubled and Troublesome: Coping with Severely Disordered Children,* London, Burnett Books

Howe, T. (1993) An Examination of the Perceptions of Pupils with Emotional and Behavioural Difficulties who have attended a residential Special School, Unpublished MEd Dissertation, University of the West of England, Bristol.

Howard League for Penal Reform (1977) *'Unruly' Children in a Human Context,* Chichester, Barry Rose

Kelly B (1992) *Children Inside: Rhetoric and Practice in a Locked Institution for Children,* London, Routledge

Keys, W. and Fernandes, C. (1993) *What Do Students Think About School?* Slough, NFER.

Lane, D. and Green, F, (1990) Partnership with pupils, in Scherer, M., Gersch, I and Fry, L. (eds.) *Meeting Disruptive Behaviour*, London, Macmillan.

Lewis A (1995) *Children's Understanding of Disability,* London, Routledge

Lloyd-Smith, M. (1993) Problem behaviour, exclusions and the policy vacuum, *Pastoral Care*, 11 (4) pp.19-24

Lunt, I. and Evans, J. (1994) Dilemmas in special educational needs: some effects of local management of schools in Riddell,S. and Brown,S. (eds.) *Special Educational Needs Policy in the 1990s: Warnock in the Market Place*, London, Routledge

Macbeath, J. and Thomas, B. (1992) The threefold path to enlightenment, *Times Educational Supplement*, 5th June

Mayet H (1992) What hope for children with learning and behaviour difficulties? *Concern* Summer No. 3

Millham S et al (1978) *Locking up Children: Secure Provision within the Child Care System,* Farnborough, Saxon House

National Curriculum Council (1989) *Curriculum Guidance 2: A Curriculum for All*, York, NCC

Norwich B (1994) *Segregation and Inclusion: English LEA Statistics 1988-1992*, Bristol, CSIE)

Pimenoff, S. (1993) What about the children? *Guardian*, 2nd February 1993

Russell, P. (1990), The Education Reform Act — the implications for special educational needs, in Flude, M. and Hammer, M. (Eds.) *The Education Reform Act 1988: Its Origins and Implications*, Lewes, Falmer Press

Saunders, S. (1994) The residential school: a valid choice, *British Journal of Special Education*, Volume 21, No.2

Scherer M, Gersch I and Fry L (eds) (1990) *Meeting Disruptive Behaviour,* London, Macmillan

Stirling M (1992) How many pupils are being excluded? *British Journal of Special Education* 19 (4) pp.128-130

Swann, W. (1985), Is the integration of children with special needs happening? An analysis of recent statistics of pupils in special schools, *Oxford Review of Education,* 11, pp.3-18

Swann, W. (1988) Trends in special school placement to 1986: measuring, assessing and explaining segregation, *Oxford Review of Education,* 14(2) pp.139-161

Tisdall, G. and Dawson, R. (1994), Listening to the children: interviews with children attending a mainstream support facility, *Support for Learning,* Vol. 9, No. 4, pp.179-183

Wade, B. and Moore, M. (1993) *Experiencing Special Education,* Buckingham, Open University Press.

Wedell, K. (1994) Special needs education: the next 25 years, in Moon, B. and Mayls, A.S. *Teaching and Learning in Secondary Schools*, Milton Keynes, Open University Press

Chapter 2

Schools by Scoundrels:
the Views of 'Disruptive' Pupils in Mainstream Schools in England and the United States

Philip Garner

Introduction

In recent years the underrated practice of listening to the views of so-called disruptive pupils has begun to assume far more importance than hitherto in both England and the United States (Cooper, 1993; Murtaugh and Zeitlin, 1989). This may in part be explained by the current emphasis in both countries on 'effective schools', one of the characteristics of which is an increased opportunity for pupil participation (Austin and Reynolds, 1990). But it is also true to say that some recent developments, in both research and practice, suggest that those schools and teachers who actively support the involvement of disruptive pupils derive significant benefits (Stevenson, 1991; Garner, 1993). Crucially, too, the academic and social performance of the disruptive pupils themselves is enhanced (Gillborn, Nixon and Ruddock, 1993).

The Context

Traditionally, very little status has been given to the accounts of schooling given by pupils whose behaviour in mainstream schools is regarded as unacceptable, especially in England (Schostak, 1983). They have been seen as a very low-status section of the school population, whose behaviour towards teachers, other pupils and to the rules and fabric of schools warrants their exclusion from any form of participation. Such pupils are frequently categorised as non-statemented in England or as nonascertained in the United States.

Pupils whose behaviour causes problems in schools have derived little protection from special education legislation, unlike formally categorised pupils: both the 1981 Education Act in England and its equivalent, Public Law 94-142 (1975) in the United States, excluded consideration of those pupils who were viewed as generally 'disruptive' or 'socially maladjusted'. Policy decisions concerning them have usually been made without their consultation or discussion with their parents, and there have been few genuine opportunities for their participation in decision-making. This has been especially so in England, where the period from the early 1970's saw hundreds of pupils referred to 'units' on an informal basis (Lloyd Smith, 1984). Far from ensuring a relevant and high-quality education for such pupils, this form of provision was heavily criticised (Lovey, Docking and Evans, 1993). One effect was further pupil-alienation from school and a concomitant reinforcement of the view that such pupils had surrendered their right to be considered as 'normal'.

The shift of ideas, or cultural transfer, between North America and England has been a long-standing feature in education (McCann, 1994). Many of the ideas 'borrowed' have assumed the level of considerable importance. In England this is especially so in special education, in its broadest sense (Carrier, 1989). North American influences are evident in such areas as assessment, developmental psychology, behaviour modification and in sociological interpretations of special education provision. In legislative terms, both the 1981 and 1993 Acts owe much to the influence of earlier developments in the United States, where the concepts of inclusivity, individual education plans and mainstreaming had a far longer pedigree (Clark, 1983). A consideration of this exchange of ideas is important in a comparative sense, in that it avoids 'assuming that developments in one country are the 'norm', and to prevent social analyses of special education becoming nationalistic or ethnocentric' (Barton and Tomlinson, 1984).

There is, however, little evidence of specific 'borrowing' in respect of recent policy initiatives for those pupils who cause problems in school. These pupils are referred to in this chapter as 'disruptive', notwithstanding the difficulties associated with such general informal categorisation (Bash, Coulby and Jones, 1985). Whilst the Elton Report (DES, 1989) referred briefly to practice in North American schools, most other cross-national references have been to aspects of curriculum and school organisation (HMI, 1990).

In the light of this it seems appropriate to investigate the views of 'disruptive' pupils in comparative terms. Both England and the United States provide historical examples of initiatives to meet the needs of this group of pupils. More recently, too, such pupils have become the focus of considerable attention by legislators and administrators, as the circulars on 'problem pupils' in England (DfE, 1994) and reports on 'students at risk' in the United States (NCEE, 1983) testify .

The historical similarities between England and the United States are considerable when comparing the general responses of both countries to 'disruptive' pupils. In both places there has been an ongoing and lively debate concerning the efficacy of segregating such pupils from mainstream provision. 'Disruptive' pupils have been traditionally viewed as threats to the established order, and attitudes appear not to have changed since the turn of the century. The 'moral panic' of the Victorian era, therefore, has been sustained in both countries, with the policy implication that school-pupils who are 'disruptive' need to be controlled because they are a threat to the stability of society (Pearson, 1983).

Investigating the views of pupils who are termed disruptive in a comparative context enables the 'threat' posed by them to be assessed in a less prejudicial manner. Problem behaviour by some pupils in schools is not simply an issue which affects a few schools in certain countries. It is a salient feature of education systems throughout the world (van Niekerk and Meier, 1994). Comparison can help to raise awareness that what is occurring, whilst being of considerable concern to teachers and others, is not indicative of a decline in standards in a given national context. It can also inform policy initiatives, at personal, institutional and national levels. Given that the recent political history of both England and the United States has been characterised by educational policies which promote 'normal' (right wing?) cultural and social values, the views of a group of 'non-normative' pupils may also help to illuminate the sharp differences between rhetoric and practice which may exist in schools. This, it has been noted, is perhaps the most fundamental cause of disenchantment in the classroom (Mongon and Hart, 1989).

The study reported briefly in this chapter records one attempt at cross national comparison. Whilst it comprises just one case-study site in each country, it nevertheless offers some suggestions that, by offering disruptive pupils the opportunity to present their views, the 'reality gap' between what these pupils think, and what teachers and others think they think, can be significantly closed. By doing this, disruptive pupils can be viewed as resources for professional and institutional development, rather than sources of stress, irritation and malevolent intent.

Gathering the evidence

Two mixed secondary schools, of approximately equal size and socio-economic catchment area, were identified as case-study sites in England and the United States. Ribbleside High School, North West England, had 670 pupils and 43 teachers. It was located in Whitebrook, a town of just over 65,000 inhabitants. In the United States, Clearwater Valley High School served Clearwater, which had a population of 57,000. Clearwater Valley had 730 pupils on roll and a teaching staff of 62.

Teachers at both schools were asked individually to provide names of those male pupils who they considered to be 'disruptive'. No explanation of the term was given to them, on the basis that such a definition is a social construction which will vary from one teacher to the next (Sacken, 1989). 74% of Ribbleside teachers and 82% of Clearwater Valley teachers responded to this request. Twelve pupils, whose names were most frequently mentioned by the staff at each school, were then identified as the target group. All were boys aged between 14 and 16. It should be added that no attempt was made to determine why individual teachers regarded certain pupils as disruptive and not others.

The views of the two groups were obtained during the course of a professional attachment (i.e. the researcher working as a teacher) in each school. Two methods of data-gathering were used. Firstly, each pupil was interviewed using a semi-structured schedule which focused upon four aspects of their school-life: the curriculum, the personal and professional characteristics of the teachers, the boys' views concerning disruptive behaviour, and the organisation and ethos of the school. Secondly, the informal comments made by the boys were recorded in a research diary, which was maintained for the duration of the research attachment. Both data-gathering instruments were tried out in a pilot study school, and confidentiality was maintained throughout by changing all real names.

The boys were given access to their own comments once they had been collated. This approach has been used by Ball (1981) in order to maintain ethical integrity within the research. This is especially important when gathering the views of marginalised individuals or groups (Jarvie, 1969). In consequence the initial willingness of the pupils to participate was revalidated at two further points in the research attachment. The pupils were also aware that they could delete or change anything that appeared in the researcher's record of their statements. This also acted as a means of validating the initial comments made by the pupils.

Prior to discussing what the disruptive pupils had to say, some mention needs to be made about the way in which the data were analysed. Individual statements were categorised as either positive (pro-school characteristic) or negative (anti-school characteristic). This was achieved by asking one member of staff from each school to classify the complete set of anonymous pupil-comments.

But it remains important not to over-analyse these pupil comments. The tendency has been for researchers to try to find a broader set of meanings from small-scale studies. It is my belief that such scrutiny detracts from the power of pupil- comment. The views of disruptive pupils should, therefore, be taken at face value, and, as I suggest in the conclusion of this chapter, can be used to effect institutional change in the school(s) concerned.

Schools by Scoundrels: the pupils' views

Some general remarks help to provide a context for subsequent category specific responses. Three main themes are apparent. The first is that, in both locations, the disruptive pupils frequently provide negative views of their experiences in school. This conforms to received wisdom about the attitudes of disruptive pupils. Thus, one English disruptive pupil, Hugh, maintained that '*teachers are all shit and they try to control you all the time'*; this depth of feeling was frequently replicated by pupils at Clearwater Valley: *'Why don't they get rid of school for guys like us....it's sick'* (Vivian). At the same time, however, there is a significant minority of pupil-statements which show that these pupils subscribe to many of the values held by the wider school community, including the teachers themselves. In this sense, the disruptive pupils in the study are by no means as oppositional to schools and teachers as commonly believed.

A second theme is that the views of these pupils tend to focus upon specific events, specific teachers or subjects and specific features of the way their school is organised. The boys are less inclined to make sweeping generalisations about schools as a whole (although there were still numerous comments such as that of Frank (Ribbleside) who aggressively complained that *'I've learnt fuck all in school. It's all crap and they're crap'*. The emphasis on more specific examples, on the other hand, lends support to the belief that individual schools do have an effect on the prevalence of disruptive pupils within them.

Finally, it is also accurate to suggest that there are more similarities between the two groups of disruptive students than there are differences. Both groups suggest that the critical point of interface is that between the individual pupil and a particular teacher. They intimate that what is important to them is the personal and professional demeanour of teachers, rather than any more general factors relating to school organisation, 'climate' or curriculum provision. Finally, the comments of the pupils imply that they are rather more willing to accept responsibility for their own actions, particularly those which relate to inappropriate or anti-social behaviour. Each of the above points will be revisited at the conclusion of this chapter.

Disruptive Pupils and the Curriculum

Little evidence is forthcoming that the pupils from both schools dislike a given subject, although when comments of this nature are made they are intensely personal and indicative of anger and frustration at having to follow a subject in which they can see little relevance. The view of Wayne at Clearwater Valley, for example, is that *'Estenson* (an English teacher) *comes round a lot and says how learning some poem's important. That's got to be fucking shit, man'*. His remark echoes that of a Ribbleside pupil,

Chris, who simply believed that *'The lesson's crap: History is a waste of time'*.

Both sets of disruptive pupils were more inclined to refer to specific subject teachers when stating their like or dislike for certain school subjects. Thus the comments by Bernard at Ribbleside that *'Mr Penny* (a Geography teacher) *does work hard and sometimes I do'* or that *'He* (the English teacher) *just gives us worksheets and then dosses about; English lessons are crap'* may be compared with that of Olwin at Clearwater Valley, who complained *'Who's Silverino* (an English teacher) *kidding when he says the work is interesting and we'll get on well if we do it?'*. To these pupils, therefore, the classroom teacher is the key factor and the personal and professional qualities which s/he manifests have a symbiotic relationship to pupil-response.

From the statements of pupils in both schools, five teacher-attributes occur with frequency. These are highlighted by the boys in both schools as being those teacher-characteristics which will be more inclined to promote learning. Teachers should therefore be:

(a) **a source of help**: *'If she helped me I think I'd be good at Geography'* (Georgie, Ribbleside); *'We don't get much attention from teachers in class so we fail'* (Steven, Clearwater Valley)

(b) **a charismatic personality**: *'I think Mrs Eden is best; she's nice and she's got a sense of humour'* (Chris, Ribbleside); *'We like teachers who give us decent work but let us have a laugh as well'* (Vivian, Clearwater Valley).

(c) **a patient person**: *'Teachers like Dimmock and Bengo expect us to learn stuff straight away'* (Ian, Ribbleside); *'Mr Mortenson is too impatient....he wants us to work too fast'* (Steven, Clearwater Valley).

(d) **a motivator**: *'Cullingford gets you working in class, because you want to for him'* (Brian, Ribbleside); *'He works real hard. Man, we come out of class and think it was great'* (Olwin, Clearwater Valley)

(e) **a disciplinarian**: *'Teachers like Bengo are crap because they've got no discipline'* (Liam, Ribbleside); *'Teachers like May have got good strict rules'* (Steven, Clearwater Valley).

The disruptive pupils also provide some insights into what for them appears to be a diet of unimaginative learning experience. Frequent reference is made to the preponderance of didactic learning, to the use of worksheets, and to the lack of suitable equipment for the boys to carry out the learning tasks. *'It* (Design & Technology) *is a lot of writing and there's no equipment'* (John, Ribbleside) and *'They expect me to do this stuff* (a worksheet) *and then wonder why I get bored'* (Olwin, Clearwater Valley) are typical examples of this perception.

There is also evidence in the comments made by the pupils that the personality of the teacher has a dramatic effect on the quality of their experience in a given curriculum area. Thus, whilst there are *'lots of subjects like Geography where you just get talked at'* (Kenny, Ribbleside), other curriculum areas are more favourably received on account of the commitment shown by the teacher, as in the case of Mr Laurie, a Science teacher, who *'says I'll make good grades in my tests. He says I will even if it kills him. He's a good guy'* (Vivian, Clearwater Valley).

Disruptive Pupils and the Personal/Professional Characteristics of Teachers

This group of pupil-statements are closely linked to those concerning their views on what constitutes a 'good' subject teacher and to their observations about discipline. It is in this section, however, that the most noticeable difference between the two groups of boys occurred. The pupils at Ribbleside tended to make comments about their teachers in general, whilst those at Clearwater Valley were rather more inclined to name specific teachers to illustrate a particular teacher-behaviour. One explanation for this may be the more widespread emphasis given, in the United States, to behaviour modification strategies. Whatever the merits or pitfalls of this form of behaviour management, the focus is upon specific behaviours rather than pupil-personality, and are thus less inclined to promote a blame-allocating ideology.

Notwithstanding this marked difference, the boys at both schools showed that they have a clear, even stylised view of the personal and professional qualities that constitute a good teacher. These can be grouped into (a) teacher technique/teaching style (b) teacher disposition (c) teacher control and (d) teacher fairness.

In the case of **teacher technique/teaching style** the boys placed a heavy emphasis upon a teacher's 'hard work', 'helpfulness', 'organisation' and 'involvement with pupils'. For example, David (Ribbleside) remarked that *'I work best when he says 'Right, this is what I want you to* *do today'*, whilst another Ribbleside pupil, Alan, added that *'Not all teachers ignore you : the good ones give you time and attention'*. A similar note is struck by the boys in the North American school.

Teacher disposition is rated highly as a characteristic, too. Here the boys indicated that their preferred type of teacher was one who listened, who was friendly and not unpredictable, and who gave them respect whilst retaining a sense of humour. *'I like teachers who tell me how it is and give me a chance to answer'*, said Norton (Clearwater Valley). Ray, also at Clearwater Valley, maintained that *'You'll never change creeps like Templeman they just don't respect us'*, and another Clearwater pupil, Vivian, made the point that *'We like teachers who give us decent work but let us have a laugh as well, so we still do okay'*. A parallel series of comments from the Ribbleside boys confirm these preferences.

The boys at both Ribbleside and Clearwater Valley maintain very fixed views about **teacher control**. They wanted teachers who dealt with behaviour problems personally, who were consistent in their application of punishments, who were strict and exhibited what one boy referred to as 'calm control'. Illustrative of these characteristics are the comments of Alan (Ribbleside) and Steven (Clearwater Valley): *'Dimmock creates a bad atmosphere in class because he's always shouting'; 'We respect teachers like May because he's strict, real strict'*.

Lastly, **teacher fairness** is the focus of much comment. The boys in both schools preferred teachers who were 'honest' (*'admitting he was wrong'*), willing to negotiate and listen to another side of the story (*'They never wait for my explanation....they don't care about my views'*, and those teachers who made sanctions fit the misdemeanour (*'Bad behaviour is not dealt with properly: sometimes you're punished for little things'*).

Disruptive Pupils and their own behaviour

In almost equal parts the boys in this study accounted for their inappropriate behaviour by one or more of the following: that the problem was my **own fault** (*'If you disrupt a lesson you deserve to get sent out'*), the **teacher's fault** (*'I fool around with those teachers who treat me like shit'*), the fault of the **school system** (*'Nothing's provided for us here, so we make our own fun like trouble'*) or **somebody else's fault**, usually a classmate or other pupil (*'Sometimes my mates wind me up'*). Within this general categorisation, some important features can be identified, which demonstrate parallels between the two groups of boys.

A high proportion of the pupil-comments were concerned with their one to one interactions with certain teachers, a point noted elsewhere in this chapter. This emphasises the importance of the personal and professional characteristics of teachers, their ability to 'make links' with this group of pupils who, it has been noted, are frequently ostracised in school. Moreover, this combined with the fact that many of the boys, in both locations, showed a willingness to accept at least some responsibility for their actions (as noted by Wayne at Clearwater Valley: '*I can be real mean sometimes and I deserve what comes back to me*') may form a useful point from which future professional development can begin.

Additionally there is evidence that the boys are aware of the doubts that some of their teachers may have about both schools' approaches to the problem caused by 'disruptive' pupils. Olwin (Clearwater Valley), for example, maintained that he knew that '*Mr Templeman doesn't like some of the rules (and) thinks they're unfair on us*'. This theme was picked up at a later stage in conversation with teachers from both schools, indicating that there was by no means universal agreement about certain aspects of the discipline codes in the schools.

Worrying, too, was the belief expressed by many of the boys that inappropriate behaviour was something to be expected from pupils: in a sense it was 'the thing to do'. So Chris (Ribbleside) took the view that '*We all like to have a go, that's natural, isn't it?*', and his friend, Liam, maintained that '*All teachers ask for it because of the job they do*'. The disruptive pupils at Clearwater Valley provide a set of comparable comments: '*It's us and them. That's the tradition....that's what's expected*' (Maury); '*Teachers will always be teachers, and us guys will always be trying to catch them out*' (Peter) are indicative of this feeling.

Disruptive pupils and School Organisation and Ethos

Once more the pupils at Ribbleside and Clearwater Valley suggest that certain teachers are important mediators between disruptive pupils and school life in general. Heavy emphasis is placed by nearly every pupil on the rules and procedures which govern their lives in school. Moreover, the boys seemed able to divorce a 'rule' or 'procedure' from the person charged with implementing it. They are therefore very conscious of status, and that some teachers can enforce rules rather more than others. George, one of the disruptive pupils at Ribbleside, stated that '*If you swear at some teachers it's alright but try it with Rayban*', whilst Daniel from Clearwater Valley maintained that when '*you get caught by Laurie you're OK, but if May sees you then it's real bad*'.

Most of the pupils in this study feel that the rules and procedures of their school are just 'there'. They do not feel as though they are able to change things. This sense of acceptance of a given status quo is frequently confirmed: '*If you do something against the rules you expect to be punished*' (Kenny, Ribbleside) and '*It's not worth fighting the rules. They're there and you can't change them*' (Danny, Clearwater Valley) are two examples of this sentiment.

Nevertheless, the boys in both schools frequently point to inconsistencies in rule application, or to the (perceived) inappropriateness (even stupidity) of some of them. Thus, one of the Clearwater Valley pupils confirmed that '*There's too many different interpretations of the rules*' (Maury), whilst one of the English pupils stated that '*You have to have a go because of the stupid rules*' (Hugh). Pupil alienation, in both schools, therefore appears to be reflected in confrontation or withdrawal.

Perhaps the most significant group of pupil-comments is that which refers to their feeling of isolation or lack of inclusion in the procedures which govern those school routines which most affect them. Lack of responsibility ('*We keep asking if they'll let us have a proper School Council with power instead of using it for fucking useless stuff like running the tuck shop*': Frank, Ribbleside), an absence of real control over what is happening to their own education ('*Teachers ought to talk with us to find out how we really think*': Bernard, Ribbleside), and an admission that they are an 'underclass' within the school community ('*There's too much division between good students and bad students*': Tommy, Clearwater Valley) are all feelings which are frequently expressed by the two groups of pupils.

Ribbleside and Clearwater Valley compared: a Summary

Over 1200 individual comments were taken from disruptive pupils at the two schools. Using the approach described in an earlier part of this chapter, these comments may be summarised in order to give a sense of the pupils 'reality' of schooling.

The disruptive pupils provide a substantial number of negative statements about what is happening to them in school, indicating disaffection in each of the four themes investigated. But a significant minority of statements suggest that such negative experiences are not universal, and that even 'disruptive' pupils express feelings of optimism about education.

In most cases, however, these thoughts are expressed using examples which are personal, drawn from contact with a small group of individual teachers. The boys suggest, therefore, that it is the actions of particular teachers which do most to colour their impression of what is happening to them. Teachers, rather than curriculum, are the substantive opinion-formers.

In the absence of any power to affect what happens to them, the boys at both schools show a remarkable ability to negotiate existing school rules and protocols. This is done to make school more acceptable, although it should not be forgotten that the boys also show that they are able to justify such subversion by pointing to the perceived irrelevance, or unfairness, of the procedures which control them. In each school, too, the boys finally demonstrate a willingness to accept some responsibility for their own actions, particularly when referring to the problematic behaviour that they engage in.

As an ancillary exercise during the fieldwork stage of this study, the views of some of the teachers in both schools were also gathered. Whilst it is not my intention to discuss this aspect of the study in detail, it nevertheless remains important to acknowledge that the views expressed by many of the teachers concurred with those provided by the disruptive pupils themselves. Thus, the teachers talked about the importance of good lesson preparation, of variety in learning tasks and the way they are introduced; they talked of non-judgmental approaches to the most problematic of pupils, of the need for sets of rules which were uniformly applied; and they also recognised the institutional and societal controls placed upon them which inhibited creative professional action to address the needs of disruptive pupils in their school. These sentiments, gathered informally, suggest that there is rather more common ground between the disruptive boys and their teachers. Certainly, a more detailed investigation may indicate that both teachers and disruptive pupils have to function in situations which are not of their own making and by no means ideal.

Ultimately, however, the comments made by the boys themselves show that there is a significant gap between what the schools say they provide and the experience of those on the receiving end. As the quest to provide inclusive education gathers pace in the 1990's, therefore, it should not be forgotten that so-called disruptive pupils can be of material assistance in helping teachers to close this gap. What these pupils say can be used by schools as data, as a critique on existing practices. And, subsequently, the disruptive pupils themselves can be 'brought back in' by giving status and respect to their opinions by providing opportunities for them to participate more positively in what goes on in school.

References

Austin, G. and Reynolds, D. (1990) 'Managing for Improved School Effectiveness: an international survey', *School Organisation*, 10 (2 & 3), 1 67-1 78.

Ball, S. (1981) *Beachside Comprehensive*, Cambridge; Cambridge University Press.

Bash, L., Coulby, D. and Jones, C. (1989) *Urban Schooling*, Eastbourne; Holt, Rinehart and Winston.

Barton, L. and Tomlinson, S. (rds.) (1984) *Special Education and Social Interests*, Beckenham; Croom Helm.

Carrier, J. (1989) 'Sociological Perspectives on Special Education', *New Education*, 11 (1), 21-31 .

Clark, M. (1983) '*Reforming Special Education: A Comparative Study of the United States and Britain*', unpublished MA thesis, University of London, Institute of Education.

Cooper, P. (1993) 'Learning from Pupils' Perspectives', *British Journal of Special Education*, 20 (4), 129-133.

Department of Education and Science (1989) *Discipline in Schools* (The Elton Report), London; HMSO.

Department for Education (1994) '*Pupils with Problems*', London; DfE.

Garner, P. (1993) Involving 'disruptive' students in school discipline structures', *Pastoral Care in Education*, 10 (3),13- 19.

Gillborn, D., Nixon, J. and Ruddock, J. (1993) *Dimensions of Discipline. Rethinking Practice in Secondary Schools* London; DFE.

Her Majesty's Inspectorate (1990) *Teaching and Learning in New York City Schools*, London; HMSO.

Jarvie, L. (1969) 'The problem of ethical integrity in participant observation', *Current Anthropology*, 10 (5), 505-508.

Lloyd-Smith, M.(ed.) (1984) *Disrupted Schooling*, London; John Murray.

Lovey, J., Docking, J. and Evans, R. (1993) *Exclusion From School*, London; David Fulton.

McCann, P. (1994) *'Transfer and Transformation : British Culture and Newfoundland Education in the Nineteenth Century'*, paper to the 16th ISCHE Conference, Vrije Universiteit, Amsterdam.

Mongon, D. and Hart, S. (1989) *Improving Classroom Behaviour: New Directions for Teachers and Pupils*, London: Cassell.

Murtaugh, M. and Zeitlin, A. (1989) 'How serious is the motivation problem in secondary special education?', *The High School Journal*, LXXII, February/March.

National Commission on Educational Excellence (1983) *A Nation At Risk*, Washington DC, US Government Printing Office.

Pearson, G. (1983) *Hooligan: A History of Respectable Fears*, London: Macmillan.

Sacken, D. (1989) 'School Disciplinary Processes', *Urban Education*, 23 (4), 323-347.

Schostak, J. (1983) *Maladjusted Schooling*, Lewes; Falmer Press.

Stevenson, D. (1991) 'Deviant Students as a Collective Resource in Classroom Control', *Sociology of Education*, 64, 127-133.

van Niekerk, L. and Meier, C. (1994) *'A Historical-Educational Survey of the Origin of Subcultures among 'Black Youth' in South Africa'*, paper to the 16th ISCHE Conference, Vrije Universiteit, Amsterdam.

Chapter 3

Out of the Spotlight:
Girls' Experience of Disruption

Jo Crozier and Judith Anstiss

Introduction

This chapter explores a concern with the fate of girls and young women in discussion about disaffection and disruption. There are two significant processes that contribute to the marginalisation of girls and maintenance of the central focus on boys. One is in the field of special provision: most of the young people out of school and in special provision on the grounds of having emotional and behavioural difficulties are boys. More boys are excluded from schools, or referred on to specialist provision which in turn predominantly caters for boys. Where statementing has been seen to be closely linked to provision, there is a cyclical process — girls whose behaviour gives cause for concern are maintained in, or get returned to, mainstream schools whatever their needs because there are very few alternatives. A study of provision in Coventry in 1990 showed the numbers of boys and girls with statements in special schools for pupils with emotional and behavioural difficulties to be 127 boys to 10 girls (Bond, 1990).

Secondly, within schools themselves, the focus of attention given to disruption is overwhelmingly on boys' disruption; the ways in which girls' learning may be disrupted by their own and others' behaviours is overlooked. The Elton Report (1989) lent legitimacy to this emphasis on boys' behaviours and contributed to the sidelining of girls and their needs. The three behaviours that the report considered to be 'more serious examples of pupil indiscipline' were 'verbal abuse' towards teachers, 'physical destructiveness' and 'physical aggression' directed at teachers. More frequently reported, and requiring response from teachers inside and outside the classroom, were such problems as 'lack of concern', 'general rowdiness', 'unruliness', 'persistently breaking rules' (p 225). The emphasis is on physical and noisy behaviour, namely behaviour that is predominantly male.

Our objective in writing this chapter is to give an account of an investigation to discover what is happening to girls in a mainstream comprehensive school. Our account focuses on three dimensions: first we raise questions about how disruptive behaviour is defined and the effect of that definition on girls. Next we discuss research conducted through an examination of school data, observation of meetings and interviews with girls. Finally we discuss the implications of our findings.

Identifying the problem

There has been significant increase in interest in girls and their schooling in recent years and this reflects girls' increasing visibility in school achievements and in taking part in their own right and on their own terms in the arena outside school (Woods, 1990, Adler, 1988, Lees, 1993, Measor and Sikes, 1992). However, in the bulk of the literature to do with disruption in schools the focus is on boys and at a day-to-day level in school the distribution of attention and resources remains disproportionately in favour of boys. The most recent guidelines from the Department for Education, Circular 9/94, acknowledge the imbalance in the provision for girls who have emotional and behavioural difficulties compared with boys with similar needs:

it is generally accepted that boys demand and obtain disproportionate teacher time, and that the needs of girls and young women are consequently often overlooked and unmet (DFE, 1994).

Girls' learning is interfered with by their own and others' disruptive activities, and this must be a cause for concern, but it is hard to keep girls on the agenda. They are rendered invisible in respect of their part as disrupters and disrupted. Measor and Sikes (1992) comment on the neglect, until recently, of girls' deviance in school. The implications from the literature on delinquency and troublesome behaviour in school would suggest that girls were neither involved in causing trouble nor affected by their experience of schooling (Adler, 1988). Lees' study of girls and sexuality gives an account of girls developing strategies to protect their sense of identity as a resistance to the 'hidden curriculum' which marginalises them (Lees, 1993).

If disruption is seen as signalling issues to the school, including those about organisation, management, curriculum and ethos, then it is important that girls are heard and their needs responded to.

The process of sidelining the needs of girls arises to some extent from the ways in which definitions are used for disruptive behaviour. Further, this depends on who does the defining. On the whole it is teachers who define what is disruptive. They do this on the basis of what interferes with their task of teaching and what they assume therefore interferes with learning. They do not easily detach themselves from that perspective to identify what may interfere with learning but not with teaching.

Part of the problem lies in the nature of questions asked about disruption. Questions that ask teachers what behaviours they find the most disruptive and that are targeted at dealing with 'the most difficult pupils' lead to a focus of attention on boys. If the emphasis of concern is shifted to look at what interferes with learning, then it is possible to retrieve some attention to what happens to girls.

The investigation

Our study took place in a large urban mixed comprehensive school serving a multi-cultural community. The school has a good record of commitment to the progress of girls in school and has mechanisms and policies to support positive approaches. There were key people in the school who recognised that there were issues to do with the distribution of attention and support to girls and who were very helpful in planning the study.

It was appropriate for us to establish a firm base of evidence at the outset, so our research took on three main areas: an analysis of school statistical evidence; an analysis of teachers' meetings in which pupils giving cause for concern were discussed; and discussions with girls themselves.

The prevailing ethos in the school, led by the senior management team, was of commitment to gender equality and concern about the experience of girls in relation to disruption. This was manifested for us in three important ways. First, we were encouraged to have access to school data that was required for the statistical analysis. Secondly, there was a welcoming attitude that enabled the close examination of school processes where it was already clear that boys dominated the agenda. The third factor was that the commitment to girls' interests of the teachers who were interested in the project was reflected in their interactions in class. This meant that girls were not only accessible to the researchers to talk to but were fairly comfortable with being in girl-only groups for discussion and with the idea of their experience being the centre of attention.

The pressure to marginalise girls is invasive. It is noteworthy that the key people in school involved in the research said that talking about girls 'feels like a luxury item'. Making time was to flow against the tide: 'we feel guilty about spending two hours talking about girls'.

Evidence from school statistics

As a starting point we compared the amount of time and attention given to boys and girls. A clear indicator of this was to be found in the school statistics that record action taken in response to disruptive behaviour. The statistics contained figures for:

> temporary exclusion for behaviour reasons
> referrals to the school behaviour support service
> referrals to a local authority behaviour support team
> referrals to the educational psychologist

What we found out from examining the statistical data was not only that boys did predominate, but also, as the table shows, the extent of the variation of referral rates for boys and girls was in a ratio of 5:1.

Table

Action taken to deal with pupil disruption by gender:

Year 1989/90	Boys	Girls
Temporary exclusions	66	2
Referral to school support service	110	34
Referral to specialist behaviour support team	8	0
Referral to educational psychologist	15	3
Total	199	39

The ratio of boys to girls was striking in terms of their respective effect on the school systems for dealing with behaviour. It was hard to believe that girls were five times less likely than boys to need attention for reasons to do with their behaviour, but there was nothing in the data that could explain the different rates of referral. We needed to look further for explanations and the next area of exploration was to look at the basis on which pupils were seen as presenting problems and the ways in which they were discussed.

Identifying 'causes for concern'

Given the limitations of the information drawn from the statistics, it was useful to look in more detail at rates of boys and girls giving 'cause for concern' in school and the ways in which concerns were expressed about these pupils.

'Triangle' meetings took place fortnightly and comprised a Year Head, one of the Deputy Heads and the Co-ordinator for Support Services. At these meetings pupils causing concern were discussed and appropriate plans were made. One of the Deputy Heads and the Co-ordinator for Support Services were keen to ensure that girls' needs were not overshadowed by the apparently more compelling needs of boys. Occasionally they pressed for whole meetings to be allocated to girls' needs — interestingly, in every such meeting an urgent issue concerning a boy took precedence.

We recorded the figures for referral of boys and girls for discussion at triangle meetings over one term, for years 9 and 10. Twenty-two boys from year 9 were listed to be discussed compared to four girls. Year 10 showed a similar imbalance with 22 boys to two girls. Thus the ratio of boys to girls claiming the attention of these meetings was even higher at 7:1.

Triangle meetings gave the opportunity to chart this disparity in more detail and to explore the ways in which pupils were discussed and interventions planned. Notes were taken at each meeting throughout the term and plans were recorded. Our analysis of these notes focused on the criteria used to identify concerns about pupils and the ways in which behaviour was described.

The discussion revealed that boys were almost invariably referred for under-achievement, reluctance to work, uncooperative and rude behaviour, bullying (victim or bully), fighting and criminal activity. Girls were most often referred for absence from school, health problems (particularly eating problems), victims of bullying, appearance (hair, dress, length of nails, jewellery), problems at home and relationships with boyfriends. It appears that boys are described in terms of their behaviour and academic performance, while girls are described in terms of their appearance and sexuality. Sexual naming (or 'slagging off') is a common problem between pupils (see, for example, Lees, 1993, Measor and Sikes, 1992) but there were also worrying examples of teachers reflecting inappropriately on girls' sexuality, e.g. 'she dresses like a tart', 'she knows more than she should'. Boys were not referred to in similar or equivalent terms.

There were other differences in the way problems about girls and boys were identified. Concerns about girls were concentrated on home, family, emotional and health matters. Classroom and learning matters were the issues discussed in relation to boys. These differences were reflected in the strategies proposed by the triangle meetings. The plans made for girls were often characterised by inaction, a wait-and-see approach. Loose and vague proposals were made, for example ' X (girl) to have weekly chats with year head'. The proposals were often related to health, family or other outside-school approaches and sometimes involved agencies outside school. Concern about boys, on the other hand, led to clearer strategies and plans of action to be carried out in school and in lessons, included more precise detail and focused on learning and behaviour in the classroom, for example 'N (teacher) to work with Y (boy) during history lessons and to talk through appropriate and inappropriate behaviours'.

Girls talking

The third aspect of the research was the girls' perceptions of their experiences. This part of the study was based on group interviews with girls who had been selected by teachers interested in the issues we were raising. They were lively informal sessions. We talked to girls about their experiences of being disruptive and disrupted and their understanding of the differences between boys and girls in this area.

There were four groups of girls, identified on the basis that they had comfortable relationships with their teachers and represented a range of attitudes and experience.

The groups were:

1. A group of year 12 girls resitting their English GCSE. In this case the topic of disruption was used as part of the course and the option of follow-up written work was available.

2. A group of year 11 girls characterised by their teacher as 'strong' girls. This meant vocal and well able to stand up for themselves.

3. A group of year 11 girls characterised by their teacher as 'quiet'.

4. A group of year 9 girls who were part of a tutor group with a teacher who encouraged them to talk and assert their ideas.

The older girls were more confident and reflective in discussion and had more to say than the youngest group. The younger pupils may have felt more constrained when talking about their own and each other's disruptive behaviour, as the group interviews included both a teacher and a researcher from outside the school.

We refer to the two year 11 groups by the categorisations that emerged in talking to them, i.e. 'hard' and 'soft'. The group who called themselves 'soft' referred to the other group as 'hard'. The 'hard' group discussed in one session their character as a group of noticeably strong young women. One of them explained this in terms of their backgrounds:

We're from rough areas, so we have to be hard.

The self-styled 'soft' girls categorised 'hard' girls as 'having older boy-friends, with money and cars'. As this section is about the girls' own accounts it seems appropriate to use their terms.

It is worth making the point that 'quiet' or 'soft' does not necessarily imply weakness. Indeed such a posture may be an efficient strategy adopted by girls to cope or to be successful in school. Stanley (1993) discusses 'quietness' as used by girls as a deliberate tactic. It serves as a way of accommodating to the demands of school: by adopting the role of 'quiet girl' in the classroom they are able to conform to expectations while in other contexts they may behave quite differently.

Talking about disruption

The four groups of girls were asked to talk about what they understood by 'disruption' and their own involvement in and reflections on disruptive behaviour.

The most frequent elements of their accounts were to do with talking unkindly about each other, mocking each other, flirting with boys and baiting teachers. The older group looked back on their own past with a sense of relish. They could be merciless and gave an account of brutal treatment dished out to a 'wimpy' boy some years before. They laughed at the memory and gave no indications of remorse in their account:

> We pushed this boy in the stream, pulled his trousers off, wrote on his face in felt pen and put his head down the loo (year 12).

This was an extreme example. In most accounts 'bitching' and 'talking" played a large part. Mocking others, especially for owning up to being an obedient child in the family, was part of the repertoire:

> They ask 'did you watch so-and-so on TV' and then mock you if you said you didn't because you had gone to bed (Year 11 soft).

> They pick on you if you have to be in early, for example if you have to be in at nine girls will say 'come out, enjoy yourself, don't worry about your parents' (Year 11 soft).

Talking was a central feature of school life for all the groups. The girls said they talked all the time, never ran out of things to discuss. The year 9 group said they talked about what they did the previous night, about TV programmes, about boys. Talking was seen as a sign of maturity, compared to the boys who were more likely to be 'just messing about'. In contrast, older girls (year 11 hard) saw messing about as an option for girls but thought they stopped sooner while boys carried on.

A frequent focus of disruptive behaviour is baiting teachers, and this figured significantly in the accounts we heard. For the younger group (year 9) 'cheeking' teachers included not doing what they were told to do, doing the opposite of what they were asked, laughing all through lessons and 'blanking teachers out' by not responding to them at all. They commented that part of the purpose of cheeking teachers was to attract boys.

By year 11 it seemed that the teachers were a more direct target of some girls' activities and they described giving teachers 'dirty looks', 'mouthing' at them and refusing to work. One described what she saw as a very effective tactic 'giving patronising smiles — this especially winds up male teachers' (year 11 hard).

Unusual, but memorable, were more extreme behaviours directed at teachers. One of the year 11 'hard' girls recounted throwing a chair, another barricaded the door so that the teacher could not enter the room, one had told a teacher to 'fuck off'.

The older girls in year 12 remembered provoking teachers by hiding their keys. A reminiscence that they laughed about was daring each other to touch a male teacher's bottom. Dubberley (1990) describes girls' accounts of using their 'sexual power' similarly in touching male teachers' bottoms and sees it as a form of resistance. The girls in Dubberley's account were relentless in their mockery of what they saw as soft male teachers and used sexual teasing effectively to upset the power relations between teacher and pupil.

A number of the girls we talked to recalled what they felt was challenging a teachers' authority by talking all through lessons and then doing all the work at home to 'prove a point', the point being that doing schoolwork and acquiescence to authority were separable.

Talking about teachers' responses

According to the Year 9 girls, chatting was the most common and persistent misdemeanour and they noted that teachers responded variously. Some teachers seemed to mind more than others and one girl suggested that women teachers minded more than men. One thought that teachers missed a lot of what they were up to in class, while others thought that teachers failed to understand that pupils could talk and do written work at the same time.

When teachers did respond to provocations they sometimes got the wrong culprit and caused offence. But teachers' failure to deal with trouble equally caused concern among pupils. Some girls from the year 11 'soft' group thought teachers did not do enough and that they should intervene more to deal with trouble. They felt that teachers should assert their role more clearly and demand respect from pupils. Both troublemakers and teachers who failed to deal with them were a cause of fury:

I feel mad with both teachers and people (year 11 soft).

The girls' accounts revealed a clear sense that teachers responded differently to boys and girls. The year 11 'hard' girls thought teachers gave boys more attention but also let them get away with a lot. One said of boys, 'It's their school, they can do what they like'.

Differential treatment between girls and boys was claimed by girls from the year 11 'soft' group:

A male teacher will tell girls 'girls don't act like that', 'girls should know better'. Boys are not expected to know better (year 11 soft).

A particular teacher gives hard boys more attention, girls feel the underperson. There's a lot of sexism there (year 11 soft).

They thought that that this may be linked with 'hardness', that a teacher would feel threatened by a boy or 'a very hard girl'. In other, rarer, cases there was a sense of girls and boys being treated the same, but it depended on the teacher.

The effects of disruption seem to range from having fun through to serious interference with work and equilibrium. The group who were most concerned and felt most interfered with by disruption were the year 11 'soft' group who felt they were least implicated in disruptive activities and most frustrated by them. To some extent they had ways of coping. One girl from this group said:

You have to cut off. I get lost in the work

However others found that disruption did interfere by interrupting lessons:

It distracts you from work, stops concentration, makes it harder to listen to what's going on (year 11 soft).

The girls felt that they were being held back, that the effect of disruption was that they were treated as if they were not there and they felt angry about it.

> I would like some more help but the teacher is having to cope with the children, they behave like children (year 11 soft).

By contrast some of the girls held the view that disruption had entertainment value and created opportunities for 'a good laugh'. Members of the older group (year 12) agreed with the point one girl made that people in the class enjoyed the entertainment and got their work done at the same time. This supports Woods' account of the significance of 'having a laugh'. He sees humour as a form of resistance to the boredom of school and as a reaction to authority (Woods, 1976).

Whether or not a pupil joins in disruptive behaviour is a factor in group membership. The 'in' crowd must avoid looking studious: to work hard is to be a creep. The year 12 group remembered their third and fourth years (years 9 and 10) when being 'hard' was much more desirable, and getting into trouble in class was the way to demonstrate it. Some of the year 11 'hard' group agreed and said that being disruptive 'proved something to the lads'.

The girls were very different in their experience of disruption. The most affected and troubled were the year 11 'soft' group and they described their irritations and frustrations that arose from the distractions caused in class and the difficulty of getting teacher attention. However there was an aspect of disruption that several described as worse and expressed strong feelings about. The behaviour that caused most disruption to learning was what people said to each other, the words that were used. Furthermore this was the disruption that was least tackled by teachers. Name-calling and hurtful talk was experienced as devastating in the classroom.

> The words — they hurt, I can't get on with work when that's happening (Year 11 soft).

Someone said that it was easier to work when there was chaos all around than it was to work when feeling hurt by the words some people said. The girls and young women that Lees studied described similar concerns, arising both from girls' 'bitching' and from boys' denigration of girls (Lees, 1993).

> When boys are throwing things I can block them out of my mind.
> When they make remarks about how girls look — 'Oh god, you're fat'
> — they can get me angry (Year 11 soft).

The girls were emphatic about the power of words to hurt and claimed that teachers did not take this problem seriously or do anything about it. Their concern with the damaging effects of what people say to each other is borne out by the shift in emphasis in the material on tackling bullying in schools that has drawn more attention to the verbal aspects of bullying. Recent classifications of bullying draw on Olweus' work to define bullying a child or young person as including when others 'say nasty and unpleasant things to him or her'. Further, bullying is happening when someone 'is sent nasty notes, when no-one ever talks to them ...when a child or young person is teased repeatedly in a nasty way' (Smith and Sharpe, 1994)

Talking about strategies for getting through

Girls clearly need strategies to get through the rigours of school life. For some feeling strong, winding up teachers and 'having a laugh' were important aspects of the school day. Others felt more vulnerable. Two strategies were described that may have served as ways of coping with the difficult aspects of school: one of these is 'wagging'. Wagging included both staying off school altogether and skipping particular lessons or parts of the day. One of the year 11 girls had wagged off school, she said, for two months, but that was unusual. The year 12 girls described wagging as common and admitted they had done it regularly, especially in their fifth year (year 11). They wagged to be with friends or to avoid lessons they did not like. They felt that little had changed:

> We missed lessons, hid in loos, behind buildings, in the same places
> the fifth years use now.

This strategy seems to be widespread. In Stoll and O'Keefe's study of truancy 72% of what were then called fifth formers admitted truanting and for many it was a social activity to be shared with friends (Stoll and O'Keefe, 1989).

The other strategy which was useful was 'being ill', and this included menstruation. Periods cause girls some genuine discomforts and embarrassments, and these are most difficult to handle for younger girls.

However they are also useful for getting out of class for a break or to avoid an activity. This was most pleasant if a girl could take a friend to 'look after' her. That made all the difference, otherwise it was 'not worth it if your friends are not allowed to stay with you' (year 12).

Retreating to the girls' toilets featured as a way of claiming a private safe space, but no longer served as a haven because the boys were prone to invading them, according to some year 11 girls.

Friendships were important in the attempt to cope with schooling and these reflected to some extent the distinction made by the year 11 of 'hard' and 'soft'. Hard girls were more likely to have close, sometimes rowdy, friendships with boys and join them in disruptive activities, though they may feel 'showed up' if caught. The ability to 'act hard' was protection against being 'picked on', which was what awaited 'weeds'. Being 'flirty' with boys invited protection (according to year 9 respondents). Year 12 girls on looking back reflected that to get noticed it was helpful to be in with the rowdy group of boys, but as girls mature so quickly and socialise outside school with older young men, a gap between boys and girls widens over the school years and girls' friendships with each other become more important. Lees (1993) sees this development as linked to girls' changing expectations and their growing critical awareness of boys' attitudes.

'Soft' girls stressed that acceptance by their group was important. Relationships between girls were crucial to provide solidarity and security, and group membership did not change very much. They were more aware of having a difficult time in school, and the defensive role of friendship was especially strong for them.

Conclusion

Our investigation confirmed that there was an imbalance in the distribution of school time and attention, with boys using up a lot of the resources of the school and in particular the resources available to support behaviour. The statistical data we gathered demonstrated this to be a persistent tendency in a school which is sensitive to equal opportunity issues and seeks to adopt positive approaches to girls. We may assume that in less favourable circumstances girls would fare at least as badly. The girls we talked to were aware of these imbalances and knew that boys got most attention from the school: 'It's their school' and 'they can do what they like'.

Further, the examination of data from meetings showed an absence of clarity about the precise nature of concerns in relation to girls' behaviour and a preoccupation with home and family factors in discussing them, while the concerns about boys were more to do with the classroom and learning within school. The ways in which pupils were talked about seemed to be determined by their sex and girls were additionally disadvantaged by a concern with their sexuality in teachers' discussions about them. Strategies to deal with problems reflected these differences, with vague plans proposed to help girls, often on a wait-and-see basis in the hopes that time would solve problems, and often referring to family or medical help. Boys were planned for more precisely, often in terms of in-class strategies and social learning programmes. These had measurable outcomes and set clear targets. These differences reflect familiar arguments about girls' experiences in school being determined by their gender role destinies.

Girls were aware and angry about their experiences. They talked about finding difficulty in attracting teacher attention and they felt that this interfered with their progress. They were angry at being overshadowed by the more demanding behaviour of boys. They were angry that teachers did not see and respond to what upset them most, which was not noise, fighting or obviously disruptive activity, but harsh words and name-calling between girls as well as from boys. The girls felt that these hurtful experiences interfered with their learning in a significant way.

There were strategies available to draw on to resist the pressures from boys, from teachers, from being overlooked. There were opportunities to 'have a laugh' and strong alliances with friends. Some girls were able to give accounts of their own disruptive behaviours and there were special techniques available to girls such as emotional outbursts, moodiness, 'turning on the waterworks'. Awareness of their own sexuality played a part in winding up male teachers in particular with 'dirty looks' or 'patronising smiles'. As well as real problems arising from menstruation — embarrassment, discomfort, mood swings — they were also well aware of the potential to exploit such female mysteries to get out of classes or provoke a teacher.

Girls are needy, disruptive and prone to problems like boys but they present less of a challenge in school. The current interest in pupils and their disruptive behaviours, particularly since the Elton Report and the subsequent studies and projects to do with enhancing behaviour in schools, has largely failed to challenge the predominant focus on boys as producers of the behaviours most likely to be talked about. Girls' disruption is linked to their gender identity and is likely to take less active forms in the classroom. Their needs get by-passed because of the criteria used to define disruption which emphasise physical and 'acting-out' behaviours.

For schools to redress the balance there needs to be a shift of focus from behaviour and control issues to concern with learning and the variety of factors and events that interfere with it. In the light of boys' pressing demands on the limited time, attention and resources available in schools, awareness of girls' needs must not be marginalised. The task for teachers includes elements that Stanworth (1983) was describing more than a decade ago: teachers need to monitor continually their attitudes and orientations in terms of challenging and stretching girls as much as boys, and in ensuring an equitable distribution of their attention. Further, they must check that their responses to pupils are not led by the greater demands of boys. Quiet pupils and pupils who seek less attention, often girls, should be noticed and encouraged. Davies (1987) sees the marginalisation of girls as deeply embedded in the curriculum in terms of the selection of what counts as school knowledge, in respect of materials and in the interactions between teachers and pupils. Solutions have to take into account all these dimensions and seek to develop girl-friendly approaches which acknowledge girls' issues and concerns, alongside anti-sexist strategies aimed at change both within and beyond the official curriculum.

As well as redressing the balances in these ways it is important to stress girls' own capacities to resist the constraints of gender roles and limitations imposed on them. Laughing, ignoring, using strategies to escape sometimes, engaging in banter, getting on quietly whatever was happening around, solidarity with each other and the level of awareness of the issues displayed in their talk were parts of a complicated repertoire of strategies that showed few characteristics of 'victim' status. The liveliness of the discussions we had with girls and their enthusiasm in talking about their experiences of disrupting and being disrupted demonstrated the ability they had to resist the negative effects of being up-staged by boys.

In looking carefully at the status of girls in schools it is worth noting and acknowledging the definite part they are well able to play for themselves in resisting marginalisation. This duality of power and powerlessness is a theme in Lloyd's account of Leith 'lassies' as active initiators (Lloyd, 1992). The girls give critical accounts of school and teachers and revel in tales of confrontations and 'bother' as a form of resistance. Lees (1993) describes girls' experiences of sexism in school and the ways in which their responses reflect changes in the roles and expectations of women and attitudes to femininity. She sees the girls in her study as challenging traditional paths and looking for opportunities and change.

There is much to be learned from hearing what girls have to say for themselves. Teachers' and theorists' views do not reflect the complexity, the detail, the level of insight, the vigour and the feelings that girls express when they talk about their experiences. Their ready response to the opportunity both demonstrates the value of asking, and also redistributes some of the attention. Reflecting on and talking to and about girls should not be seen as a 'luxury item'. They deserve an equal place in the spotlight.

References

Adler, C. (1988) 'Girls, Trouble and Schooling' in Slee, R. (ed) *Discipline in Schools: a curriculum perspective* Melbourne, Australia, Macmillan

Bond, J. (1990) *Gender Equality in Special Education: the experiences of girls in special schools*, unpublished M.Ed dissertation, University of Warwick

Davies, L. (1987) 'Viking Wives at Home: sexism and deviance in school' in Booth, T. and Coulby, D. (eds) *Producing and Reducing Disaffection*, Milton Keynes: Open University Press

DES (1989) *Discipline in Schools: Report of the Committee chaired by Lord Elton*, London: HMSO

DFE (1994) *Circular no. 9/94 The Education of Children with Emotional and Behavioural Difficulties* London: DFE Publications Department

Dubberley, W. S. (1993) 'Humour as Resistance' in Woods, P. and Hammersley, M. (eds) *Gender and Ethnicity in Schools* London: Routledge

Lees, S. (1993) *Sugar and Spice: sexuality and adolescent girls* London: Penguin

Lloyd, G. (1992) 'Lassies of Leith talk about bother' in Booth, T. et al (eds) *Curricula for Diversity in Education* London: Routledge

Measor, L. and Sikes, P. (1992) *Gender and Schools* London: Cassell

Stanley, J. (1993) 'Sex and the quiet schoolgirl' in Woods, P. and Hammersley, M. (eds) *Gender and Ethnicity in Schools* London: Routledge

Stanworth, M. (1981) *Gender and Schooling: a study of sexual divisions in the classroom* London: Hutchinson

Smith, P. and Sharpe, S. (1994) *School Bullying: Insights and Perspectives* London: Routledge

Stoll, P. and O'Keefe, D. (1989) *Officially Present* London: Institute of Economic Affairs

Woods, P. (1976) 'Having a laugh' in Hammersley, M. and Woods, P. (eds) *The Process of Schooling* London: Routledge and Kegan Paul

Chapter 4

Perceptions of Exclusion by Pupils with Special Needs

Susan de Pear

The research on which this chapter is based set out to understand the phenomenon of exclusion, particularly of those pupils with special needs, from mainstream schools. Evidence was gathered in the form of pupils' perspectives of their educational experience prior to exclusion and the views of their teachers. The aim of the study was to discover why the present educational system apparently operates in such a way as to marginalise some of the most vulnerable of its clientele. For the purposes of this chapter the emphasis will be on what the youngsters had to report.

Past rationales of exclusion from mainstream school often attributed causes to the pupils themselves or to legislation. It is hoped that the data recorded here helps to dispel the myth that the pathology lies within the children who, given the chance, are only too willing to voice their own perspectives on seemingly inadequate educational experiences. Similarly, the teachers interviewed described a suboptimal system, rooted in control and within which any attempt at advocacy would be fought off by the prevailing culture. It is a system which produces disaffected, excluded youngsters as part of its waste. The concluding discussion advocates the creation of a culture that would enable and encourage pupil advocacy so that valid intervention could be formulated and implemented.

A large number of professionals involved with the care and the education of children have experienced frustration and anger at the exclusion of 'problem' pupils who have had little chance for advocacy and who have been denied appropriate resources and provision. Exclusion is at the end of the disciplinary line for both the educators and the individuals being educated. Unfortunately the behavioural problems of some pupils with special educational needs cause schools to deal with the situation in a purely linear way. The pupils seem to be labelled early on and the school procedures act upon them in such a way that exclusion seems inevitable. Some youngsters appear to feel so powerless in academic terms that they turn to disruptive behaviour as the most feasible form of defence in the uncomfortable situations in which they find themselves. The objective of the research was, therefore, to discover why we treat these pupils as 'naughty rather than needy' (ACE, 1992) and as a problem rather than as a challenge to our professional expertise.

Interviews were conducted with six pupils who had been referred to special school following exclusion from their secondary schools. As they had learning difficulties, the interview was deemed to be the most appropriate method of eliciting their experience and perceptions. The interviews were taped so as to guarantee concentration and the observation of 'cues', to allow both parties to relax and develop a rapport, and to ensure that the data was a true record of the pupils' perspectives, not subjective note-taking. All the interviews were painstakingly transcribed before being analysed. Lastly, anonymity was assured. When the interview appointments were made only two provisos were stipulated: (i) that each of the six interviewees had been excluded from mainstream school, and (ii) that he/she had been identified as having special educational needs.

Unstructured interviews were carried out during a pilot study and they highlighted the emphasis placed on interpersonal relationships by all those being interviewed. These relationships emerged as crucial factors in the exclusion process. Consequently, as the questions prepared for the main research needed structure as well as an emphasis on interpersonal needs, it was decided to refer to Schutz's (1966) three-dimensional theory of interpersonal behaviour, and use the FIRO-B, (Fundamental Interpersonal Relations Orientation — Behaviour) as a framework for the interviews. Questions were asked which would elicit the pupils' self-conceptions with regard to their wanted and expressed need for:

(a) *inclusion* — the need to feel significant and worthwhile e.g. *Which group would you have liked to be part of at school? Who thinks that you are significant? Why do you think that is?*

(b) *control* — the need to feel that one is a competent, responsible person e.g. *When did you feel responsible in school? Who trusted you? Who thinks that you are good or competent at something? Why?* and

(c) *affection* — the need to feel that the self is loveable e.g. *Who paid attention to you at school? What methods did you use to get noticed or to be liked? How comfortable are you showing affection? Do you like to be important to someone?*

This framework also proved a useful tool for the purpose of analysis and the identification of key traits of those most at risk from the exclusion process, as will be seen later. The method used for identifying the recorded categories of answer might not have matched exactly the FIRO-B test papers but they were a consistent interpretation, which enabled scores to be produced indicating the pupils' *wanted* and *expressed* need for inclusion, control and affection. To illustrate the analysis process there follows an example of each identified category drawn from the transcribed dialogues:

Wanted Inclusion:
Pupil A: 'They (the teachers) were more interested in clever people who were good in their lessons but what they didn't see was that if they'd just come and paid me a bit of attention I would've just sat down and done my work like everyone else.'

Expressed Inclusion:
Pupil F: 'They (his gang) didn't look up to me or down to me. They just thought I was one of them .'

Wanted Control:
Pupil E: 'I hated reading aloud and they made me read out loud which makes me stutter a bit when I'm reading. I could read when I went there

but the only thing I couldn't do was spell. Because I couldn't spell my writing was a bit scruffy. When they made me read out loud they graded me. They classed me as a- a- a- (stutter) 12 or 11 year reading age. When I could sit here quietly, by myself, and read the whole book but I couldn't read it if it was out loud. Because they grade you by your reading out loud they won't believe you if you say you can read.'

Expressed Control:
Pupil D: 'I do remember being praised at Middle School. I was really good at maths and I did tons more than the others and once the teacher said I was 'a real mathematician'.'

Wanted Affection:
Pupil B: 'I get jealous sometimes 'cos he (father) gives them (young stepsisters) money, takes them on holiday. I've never been on holiday with him. He said he'd take us after Christmas... he says he'll do a lot, but he never does.'

Expressed Affection:
Pupil C: 'The H.E. teacher did — that's the only teacher I liked. She'd help me with my food and my cooking and that, tell me what to do. That's the only teacher I liked in the whole school. That was the only lesson I was good in. That's the only teacher I was nice to. She'd be nice to me and I would be nice to her. That was it.'

Initial analysis using the FIRO criteria showed that with the first dimension of need, inclusion, without exception, the pupils scored higher on *wanted inclusion* than *expressed inclusion*. As inclusion refers to one's general social orientation, the high wanted scores mean the pupils have a strong need to belong and to be accepted. The lower *expressed* scores suggest the pupils are generally uncomfortable around people and will tend to move away from them. This evidence highlights a conflict of emotions for pupils with special needs in the context of the classroom. We might hypothesise that, having been labelled and marginalised by their learning difficulties, they have a strong wish to feel significant and be accepted academically, but that their inherent fear of failure keeps them distanced from other learners. In turn, this tension causes them either to withdraw or, as in most cases of exclusion, to act out their frustrations — on their own or with a small group of similar types.

All the pupils interviewed appeared to be *oversocial*, seeking attention incessantly. This is epitomised by one boy who stated quite honestly: 'I'm attention-seeking — I know all the blinking rules to get it!'

When considering the second dimension of need, control, the results, with a single exception, show the same pattern. The pupils' high *wanted control* scores suggest abdication of responsibility and lack of leadership behaviour. The lower *expressed* scores indicates that the pupils avoid making decisions and avoid taking on responsibility. These are in Schutz' terms, *abdicrats*, those who are not able to take responsibility or make decisions regarding their emotional or educational lives but who need to feel that they are competent, responsible persons. The interview transcripts show the significance of worthwhile pursuits that the excludees engage in outside school, for example, childminding, bar work and catering, and the pleasure a feeling of competence gives. On the other hand the data tells us of incidents in school where the feeling of incompetence caused these vulnerable youngsters to lose control, as with one who threatened a teacher with a stool, a girl, who actually threw a chair at a teacher and another boy, who admitted having been deliberately loud and extremely rude.

The third area of analysis concerned the data relevant to the pupils' need for affection — that is to say, deeper relationships. Overall the scores were lower than in the other categories due to the fact that questioning focused mainly on the educational environment. Half the pupils appeared to be *overpersonal* which seemed to indicate a fear of rejection and a strong need for affection. Most of the pupils showed a lower *wanted* score which might indicate (according to FIRO-B) that they are very selective about with whom deep relationships are formed. Although the higher *expressed* need for affection scores would normally suggest persons who would readily become emotionally involved with others, in this case it would be a mistake to draw such conclusions for, often, these high scores were due to repeated mention of one favourite friend, relative or teacher. They appear to feel quite isolated and vulnerable and the majority admit to having reduced their network of friends to just a few, if not one, trusted friend. In the past most of them have been let down emotionally and have found it a painful experience One might surmise that this has made it difficult for them to trust anyone else — especially in terms of a close interpersonal relationship.

Case Studies

Pupil A was statemented at eleven years when she had a reading age of seven. Her one area of achievement was horse-riding. Prior to her transition from middle school, difficulties in interpersonal relationships were obvious and her once cheerful nature was replaced by a sense of failure. The first signs of antagonism and lack of self-esteem manifested themselves at the end of her parents' marriage. She blamed her father whom she 'hated' and lost much following the divorce, including her beloved horse. She began her secondary schooling and immediately manifested excessive disruption and avoidance tactics especially when feeling vulnerable to criticism. However, she proved to be a fine athlete and behaved well in other lessons where her needs were addressed:

> I liked English because she didn't make me feel a fool, and make me stand up in front of everyone and read. She used to sit me on the computer to do it.

She was often on report and subject to several temporary exclusions before a final unacceptable incident (swearing at a teacher) led to permanent exclusion.

Outside school she was involved in joy-riding and under-age sex with a young man who, in her words, was 'a vicious bloke'. She got pregnant for she 'would have done anything to leave that school,' and generally cost her mother and the various authorities vast amounts of time, money and concern. From special school, where she has learned to accept help and has plans to go into further education, she reported her feelings of remorse but also her feeling of anger towards the school which excluded her when she stated: 'I'm going to prove them wrong — I'm going to make something of my life!'

Analysing Pupil A according to the FIRO criteria, she scored reasonably high on both *wanted* and *expressed inclusion*, thus appearing to be *oversocial* — making people pay attention to her. Scoring high on *expressed control* and low on *wanted control* suggests she is an *autocrat*, wanting to dominate others. This was manifestly true both in and out of school especially at the time of the first interview. Lastly, the affection area is painful for her as she has been rejected by her father and her first boyfriend. Her extremely low *wanted* and *expressed affection* scores can be interpreted to indicate someone *underpersonal* whose responses are extreme, being motivated by a strong need for affection and an anxiety about being unlovable.

Pupil B was thirteen with a reading age of an eight year old. She was from a broken home and felt jealous of her step-siblings and the attention paid to them by her absent father. She felt both were reasons enough for 'being naughty':

> It was her (mother) that used to have all the boyfriends....They used to move in and move out I used to come into school in a really big mood and scream at all the teachers.

> He (father) don't take no notice of us. He just wants to know the little ones (twin step-sisters), they're seven.

Attention seeking and apparent labelling by teachers both caused her to act out:

> They always used to think I was naughty so I made myself be naughty.

Unfortunately Pupil B felt isolated and untrustworthy, she had little opportunity to discuss her problems and when she did she found it difficult:

> We used to be in a little office like this ...and I just used to look around and not listen to her (support teacher). I just didn't want to know.

> I do see him a bit at the moment. I don't really talk to him (father).

> I apologised but nobody (teachers) said nothing except 'You'll be gettin' a detention'.

> Just Zoe (former mainstream friend), I told Zoe everything. I don't talk to no-one any more.

At the time of the interview she had recently started at the special school, joining her elder brother who had formerly been excluded. She talks of him as her favourite person saying they stood up for each other in times of need:

> Me and my brother get on close. He sticks up for me and I stick up for him. This other boy just bruised him. . . and I got hold of him and punched him!

In terms of the FIRO analysis, Pupil B, with her high *wanted inclusion* score and her exhibitionist behaviour, appears to be an *oversocial* type. Her primary goal would be to gain attention. The low *expressed control* and high *wanted control* characteristics suggest an *abdicrat* type who feels incapable of responsible, adult behaviour. She has quite high *wanted* and *expressed affection* scores indicating she is *overpersonal* with anxiety about being rejected and unloved.

Pupil C had been excluded in Year 9 and was out of school for over a year before being given a place at special school. He was fifteen when interviewed. Apart from one good relationship with an H.E. teacher he had felt 'out of place' at school because:

> The teachers never took no notice of you. They always go up to the clever people. The people that were not very clever ....they just leave them.

He did not want to leave his school but:

> Because I was a pain, a nuisance, naughty, kept swearing — they chucked me out.

He, too, was from a broken home and his irresponsible and at times reckless behaviour had caused his mother to fence him in and be overprotective, although he understood her motives. When his Dad left home he 'missed him all the time' but knew that he was 'his best mate.' He still had a good relationship with him and saw him on a regular basis but missed his stepsister whom he 'loves to death' but did not see. He gained the respect of his small group of friends by daring acts such as jumping off the school roof and being 'brilliant on computer games.' He said that at the arcade:

> They show me off 'cos I'm so good ... I'll beat anyone.

At school it was a different matter. He felt 'stupid' going to special classes in the learning support room; he felt that he got attention only when he was naughty; he felt 'pissed off' about his unfair exclusion because, 'they just didn't want me'.

Pupil C's *wanted* and *expressed inclusion* scores are reasonably high indicating a feeling that no-one is interested in him and a desire to gain attention. His high *wanted control* and lower *expressed control* suggests an *abdicrat* who likes a subordinate position and avoids situations where he might feel incompetent or stupid. This matches his description of his school experience exactly — especially his wish for secrecy when going to the special needs room for lessons. He seems to be a *personal* type according to the *affection* scores, for although he has a high *expressed* need (for his Dad, his step-sister and the H.E. teacher) his *wanted* need is average, probably because he knows that people who know him well respect and admire him. He is also capable of giving genuine affection.

Pupil D had been out of mainstream for nearly a year without any home tuition. The interview was short as he did not seem as comfortable talking to me as the others and when there was an interruption by a teacher, he took the opportunity to say he did not want to miss the next lesson. He would rather be back in his mainstream school, felt he should not be at the special school, and that his exclusion for swearing at a teacher was unfair. He considered himself good at maths but knew he had problems with copying off the board in English:

> I could've got some of it done but what was the point if I never finished it?

Although he says he was supposed to have been a bully at his old school he also perceived himself as 'the class clown':

> I didn't do nothing really bad, I got bored and messed about and made my mates laugh. I'd go back but I don't know how I'd get on with the work.

His parents were not sympathetic — in fact they took little interest in him and the rest of the family treated him quite badly The only feeling of importance he remembered was when his Dad's boss showed him respect 'a few years ago'.

His *wanted* and *expressed* scores for *inclusion* were both high, indicating an *oversocial* type who is exhibitionist and seeks attention from others. His high *wanted control* and extremely low *expressed control* suggests an *abdicrat* — incapable of responsible, adult behaviour. With virtually no *affection* scores he appears to be *underpersonal* — avoiding closeness and feeling vulnerable to rejection.

Pupil E was fourteen and had been excluded twice with a short period in mainstream in between. He was not sure why he had been excluded:

I don't know, I think it was my work, and maybe a bit of a behaviour problem.

He had had 'enough moving around schools', felt unfairly assessed, and would like to be part of a mainstream school again providing he could cope. He admitted attention-seeking tactics saying that if teachers did not pay attention he 'had a go at them' and 'didn't do nothing' whereas:

If I had attention I'd feel better. I could write a thousand words in a minute.

He felt that he was a scapegoat for others' bad behaviour in mainstream and that they did not give him a chance to settle in before removing him. He appeared to be a loner with practically no friends his own age and only one or two teachers to whom he had ever related. He mentioned people he met on holiday as best friends and said he was important to them because he made them laugh:

It's boring but with me around...I can cause a bit of havoc, a little bit of fun

His one responsibility in school was collecting the litter. He seemed lacking in self-esteem generally, but tried often during the interview to cover this up. For example, when asked if there were times when he felt unimportant, answered:

Yeah loads of times but mainly I didn't take a blind bit of notice.

He reported being nervous, always sitting with his back against the wall, saying: 'I don't feel safe.' His family background is complicated: his parents are separated and he spends time in both households. He seems close to his grandparents and to both parents, although:

My mother listens to me but she's always too close to the flipping telly!

Two-thirds of the way through the interview, when he seemed to trust me, he told me about his beloved big brother who choked and died after a drinking bout a few years ago. He has clearly never got over the loss of his 'best' brother and misses him 'totally'. He still cries every night:

It's like bottling it up, till about twelve o'clock at night, every night, you know.

His grief obviously affects his behaviour at school:

> It makes me feel sad but in a funny way it makes me behave like a vicious dog — everybody gets a snap.

Pupil E is *oversocial* having the top scores for both *wanted* and *expressed inclusion*. Like all the pupils analysed so far, he has an underlying feeling that no-one is interested in him so he is constantly attention-seeking. In his words, he 'knows all the blinking rules to get it!' With extremely high *wanted control* and extremely low *expressed control* he is a definite *abdicrat*, liking subordinate positions (e.g. litter collector) and feels incapable of adult behaviour or of taking things seriously — apart from the death of his brother. One could speculate that this event has so traumatised him that he finds concentration and competence impossible and so 'loses' himself in his position as a joker. His reasonably high *wanted* and *expressed affection* scores suggest that he is *overpersonal*, tending to be intimate and confiding. In his transcript there is mention of being able to keep secrets. Because his initial experiences with affection have turned out badly (in terms of his parents' separation and the loss of his brother) he perhaps feels that if he tries hard things may turn out better.

Pupil F is in Year 11 and has been excluded from two schools, having been in trouble for most of his time in secondary school. He reported being 'fine' in junior school, the problems beginning in secondary school due to 'mixing with the wrong people' and the fact that the teachers did not know him — a common experience of youngsters making the transition between schools. He blamed his last exclusion on the powerful influence of his peer group who, although being mutually supportive, he described as 'the loud group — people who didn't work'. These pupils disrupted lessons and rarely did as they were told. He was not the leader, just 'one of them' and although they all damaged a lift he was the only one excluded, confirming his perception of being the scapegoat — unfairly targeted by half of the teachers:

> Yeah, anything I'd done, they'd be on my back: shouting at me, screaming, throwing me out of class. But the thing was, it was only me that it happened to.

Working in class depended on the teachers — whether they liked and trusted him or not. Like all the excludees interviewed, he reported that the respect that the teachers showed him was crucial in terms of the behaviour that he would manifest. This pupil's transcript also highlighted different types of teaching style, which might be characterised by the terms coined by Jordan (1974), 'deviance-provocative', or 'deviance-insulative' (cited in Hargreaves et al 1975). For example, Pupil F imagined what some teachers said about him in the staff room and really believed that they tried to get him into trouble, thus fuelling a self-fulfilling prophecy:

> I'm sure the teachers used to sit in the staff room and say, 'Well I've got him next lesson, I'll start on him!' Just to get me into trouble. I'm sure they used to do that.

When asked to describe the teachers he would work for, he replied:

> The ones I worked for were all right because they didn't used to shout at me. Like if I was talking and they'd say, 'Can you be quiet or stop talking while I'm talking?' I used to agree with that — but most teachers just shout, 'Shut up! Don't talk!' So I used to have a go at them and then we'd have an argument and I'd get thrown out.

However, some were 'deviance-insulative' and in his words: 'If they treat me nice, I treat them nice'. Others seemed unwittingly to play on his fear of failure when asking questions that he could not answer:

> I feel stupid when a teacher says something and I can't think of an answer, when they're all laughing at me.

As an *abdicrat* he feels incapable of responsibility and tries to avoid situations where he feels stupid. Likewise, the trust shown by teachers influences behaviour. It was depressing to note that several of the excludees could only remember a single example when they had been trusted or given responsibility by a teacher, none of them, incidentally, being academic pursuits. In this boy's case, it was shopping for his French teacher.

Pupil F admits to having a conscience following disruptive incidents and when asked if it was generally peer pressure that made him act in such a way, answered:

> Yes, especially when there are five of them going on at me, 'You boffin' getting on with your work.' So I used to think, right, I'm not going to do no more.

He seemed at the interview to be a sensible and sensitive young man who had hope for the future and had decided on a career as a chef. He realised a little late that, due to his exclusions and behaviour, he had been 'falling behind' with his education:

> At first it's just a laugh but when you think back, you think, 'I should've *been* there, *done* it'.

This last pupil is similar to most of the others interviewed in that he, too, comes from a broken home. At the time of the trouble at school he lived with his father. He is now residing with his mother and much younger step-siblings whom he resents:

> If anything goes wrong in the house it's down to me ... it's my fault.

However he admitted that things were working out a lot better with his mother although he was worried, as he has not seen his dad since he was excluded and if left alone:

> I can sit down, on my own, and think about him. Like, I don't know where he is, whether he's still alive ... but if I'm with other people I don't really care.

He needs to talk about his problems with a trusted person but says he has not found that person yet. However, he has at last found relative happiness at the special school because:

> Everyone knows everyone, no-one hates anyone here, everyone likes each other — which is the best part. It's really good.

According to his high scores for *wanted* and *expressed inclusion*, this pupil is clearly *oversocial*, and like the other excludees would seek others incessantly as he hates to be ignored. With an underlying feeling that no-one was interested in him, his response would be to *make* people pay attention to him. His very high *wanted control* and lower *expressed* score suggest he is an *abdicrat* and so he feels incapable of responsibility and tries to avoid situations where he feels stupid. His high scores on *wanted* and *expressed* need for *affection* indicate that he is *overpersonal*, being motivated by a fear of rejection and a strong need for affection.

Discussion

The data show that it might not be the fact that these pupils had no wish to take responsibility in the learning situation but that some teachers dealing with them, prior to exclusion, gave them little opportunity to succeed. There were comments such as: 'You get shoved to the back of the class', 'The teachers never took no notice of you', 'They won't believe you if you say you can read' and 'Teachers don't help you when you put your hand up.' These provide evidence of the frustration and powerlessness that they felt in school. Evidence from the teachers regarding the importance given to control issues is confirmed by the pupils who report that some teachers seem to be 'deviance-provocative' (Jordan 1974, cited in Hargreaves et al 1975) in that they presume that classroom contact is a battle of wills and that pupils do not want to work. Half the excludees mention this tendency in their interviews.

The negative effects of low self-esteem and the link between self-esteem and the sense of competence and achievement are now widely recognised. Thus the task of special needs educators, must be to instil in pupils a feeling of self-worth and show that, whatever the level of their academic achievement, their efforts and opinions are valued and they are valued as persons. Effective, caring teachers know already that what these pupils need is to be included in the learning process and not marginalised, something recognised by Pupil A:

> I didn't like Mrs B., I hate her. I like Mrs M. Mrs M used to talk to me like I was a proper human being. She used to talk to me like she used to talk to everyone but Mrs B she used to get up close to me and screw up her eyes and talk through her teeth to me.

Two of the most interesting findings of this research have been the facts that practically all of the excludees have indicated that in their view it was never too late to undo what had gone before and that they would prefer to be in mainstream school. The following extract serves to illustrate this point and suggests, sadly, that they think that they will not 'fit into' mainstream school until they themselves improve.

> **Pupil C**: ... but I'm getting cleverer and if I'm, like, really smart like all the other kids in mainstream school, I'd go back there. It'd be really good. It'd be great.

SdP: So you think that being smart is how you'd fit into school? The only way?

Pupil C: Yep!

The experiences recounted by the pupils often reflected institutional processes involving the attribution of certain characteristics which in turn shaped behaviour. This attribute-driven view of the world manifested itself in repeated references to the impact of being labelled as 'remedial' or 'disruptive' and targeted as a trouble-maker. These processes were recognised by the pupils themselves as being self-fulfilling and caused much resentment with half the excludees mentioning being 'picked on' unfairly. This echoes the evidence from Tattum's study of disruptive pupils in special units (Tattum 1982), for example:

> **Pupil B**: Yes....it was because I had the bad name. Because my sister and my brother went to this school and well like they think 'cos they were naughty and got expelled they put it on my name.

> **SdP**: Really?

> **Pupil B**: When I went to P.E., the teacher turned round to me and said, 'Oh no, not another E.! (surname). This got on my nerves. It started from there. I started being naughty. They always used to think I was naughty so I made myself be naughty.

The powerful effect of teachers' expectations on pupil outcomes has been known for a long time (Holt 1966, Nash, 1973) and supporting evidence for this can be seen in the cases of these excluded pupils who seemed to have had little incentive to behave appropriately. In fact, by not doing so, these pupils seemed to get what they wanted: attention from the teachers and kudos as the class clown, deviant or bully. This was also a distancing factor, for once marginalised they found it impossible to re-integrate themselves.

As will have been noted, five of the six pupils came from broken homes, a factor frequently assumed to be a sufficient explanation of troublesome behaviour in school. However, Lloyd-Smith (1984) has pointed to the danger of giving 'family-based pathological explanations' for problem behaviour. He states that the 'ubiquitous medical model' has often been 'uncritically applied to social problems' which diverts attention away from other important factors and can lead to the amplification of the original problem in a self-fulfilling way. In the case of the excluded pupils, if we blame dysfunction in the family we are missing the point. The fact that many pupils from broken homes perform well in certain educational settings means that it is to the system in school that we must look for a full understanding of disaffection. The data would seem to indicate that the two-fold disadvantage of family trauma and learning difficulties makes pupils more vulnerable to the processes in the school system which lead to exclusion.

Cooper and Upton's (1991) ecosystemic model suggests that contributions to disruptive classroom behaviour could be made by all participants, including the teacher, and that all perspectives on any particular incident should be valued. In the case of 'incident slips' collected prior to exclusion in many schools, it is rare to see any record of the child's view of the circumstances. Where pupils with special needs are involved it would seem appropriate that examples of set tasks should be attached so that any mismatch between ability and expectations could be recognised. One pupil's transcript gave evidence of this sort of discrepancy when, having unsuccessfully tried a task and having failed to get the help he wanted because the teacher was helping the 'smart kids', he used to rip up his work or 'scribble over it.'

What might have made a difference would have been a chance for such pupils to voice their feelings. Overall, however, opportunities to indulge in self-advocacy were seen to be rare. The Code of Practice for Special Needs (DfE, 1994) recommends pupil advocacy as a part of the review stages. It must be hoped that of all the recommendations this one will be followed. How much more could pupils be achieving if they were involved in their learning, if we listened to their needs, if we allowed them to make sense of any barriers or problems, and if we gave them more control over their acquisition of competence? These vulnerable youngsters need to feel they are valued, that what they have to say about their learning is paid attention to, and that future planning of their access to the curriculum is a negotiated process of which they feel some ownership.

References

Advisory Centre for Education (1992) Exclusions. *ACE Bulletin* No 45, 9- I0.

Cooper, P. and Upton, G. (1991) Controlling the urge to control: an ecosystemic approach to problem behaviour in schools. *Support for Learning* 6 1, 22-26

Department for Education (1994) *Code of Practice on the Identification and Assessment of Special Educational Needs.* U.K.: Central Office of Information.

Hargreaves, D. H., Hester, S. K. and Mellor, F. J. (1975) *Deviance in Classrooms,* London, Routledge and Kegan Paul

Holt, J. (1966) *How Children Fail,* London: Pitman.

Lloyd-Smith, M. (ed) (1984) *Disrupted Schooling,* London: John Murray.

Nash, R. (1973) *Classrooms Observed,* London: Routledge and Kegan Paul.

Schutz, W.C. (1966) *The Interpersonal Underworld,* USA Science and Behaviour Books Inc.

Tattum, D. (1982) *Disruptive Pupils in Schools and Units,* Chichester: John Wiley

Chapter 5

A 'Dunce's Place': pupils' perceptions of the role of a special unit

Anne Sinclair Taylor

This chapter sets out to describe the functioning of a 'special' unit in a comprehensive school from the children's and teachers' perspectives. It will focus on what they think the purpose and role of the unit is and analyses how this affects one of its formal purposes, that is, promoting integration between mainstream and unit pupils. To put this material into context there will be some discussion about the genesis of unit provision, followed by a description of the school in which the study took place. The chapter will also refer to the techniques used for data gathering, and ethical questions raised.

Units and integration

Educational policies which promote the integration of pupils with 'special needs' into mainstream schools have been increasingly pursued in the United Kingdom since the early 1960s. Some local authorities have sought to facilitate educational integration by setting up 'special' units attached to mainstream schools. Unit provision takes many forms and serves different purposes. However it can be argued that units attached to mainstream schools provide a buffer between 'special' and ordinary provision and allow their pupils the best of both worlds: the protection or special care of the special school and the wider social and academic opportunities available in mainstream education. An on-site unit provides not only 'locational' integration, to use the terminology of the Warnock Committee (DES, 1978a), but also 'social' integration, with lunch breaks and playtimes providing scope for informal interaction and social mingling.

Research into how units operate is timely, since recent draft circulars have raised important questions about the status and funding arrangements for unit provision, already in existence, as well as for the development of Pupil Referral Units for excluded pupils (DFE, 1993). This chapter focuses on a 'free standing' unit, that is one which is on a mainstream campus but whose pupils are on roll in the unit, not the host school. Such units are expected to 'in future become part of a host school' (DFE, 1993 p.21). It will be argued in this chapter that the success of these developments will rest, at least in part, on careful monitoring which includes the investigation of participants' understandings and experiences of integration.

Integration is a concept which is understood and interpreted differently; in this sense it might be described as an 'essentially contested' concept (Gallie, 1955-6 p.167). Typologies such as the Warnock Committee's, already referred to, have evolved to help clarify and communicate meanings. However, it is probably most helpful to think in terms of a continuum of experience. Wade and Moore (1992) have developed a model which ranges from separation, where the child lives in a completely segregated hospital setting for example, to integration where provision is made for all pupils with special needs in mainstream classes (p9). While each child responds in an idiosyncratic way to the structures which individual schools put in place to facilitate integration, further complex and interacting influences affect developments. These include LEA and host school perspectives among others. This chapter will refer to the ways in which local conditions interacted with the implementation of integrative policies in a specific school.

Previous research into unit provision has focused on curriculum opportunities for pupils and reintegration rates following unit placements (see for example. DES, 1978b; Davies and West, 1985; OFSTED, 1993). In contrast, few studies have examined the social integration of unit and mainstream pupils; those that have, such as Hurford and Hart, 1979, and Lowden, 1985, show disappointing levels of interaction and friendship building between pupils from units and those from mainstream. Even less in evidence are the views of unit pupils about their experiences of schooling.

Research at Limeleigh Comprehensive

The research for this study was based at Limeleigh comprehensive; a three form entry, multicultural, inner-city school. An ethnographic approach was adopted where the researcher shares, as far as possible, the same experiences as the subjects and where acceptance by the group being studied is essential (Hammersley, 1986, Bell, 1987). Previous inspections of the unit by HMI and the LEA had been critical of its management and emphasised the need for greater integration between mainstream and unit. The unit's curriculum was described as superficial and unrelated to the host school's syllabus.

As the research developed, it emerged that these inspections had been used as part of a strategy by the head of the school, to 'shake the place up'; one member of staff being a particular target. My involvement, at the invitation of the head, was to continue with that process. This began to raise ethical issues about my presence and the purpose, process and outcomes of the research. As one teacher in Stephen Ball's study of a comprehensive school says, 'should you (the researcher) have the right to do a sort of carve up job on a teacher?' (Ball, 1984 p.85).

According to Bulmer (1980), 'Ethics is a matter of principled sensitivity to the rights of others'. How far should one person's rights be seen as more important than another's; for example where a teacher's actions are detrimental to a pupil's educational and social opportunities? Some researchers argue that there is a responsibility to give a voice to those who have least opportunity to express their ideas, that 'The institutionally powerful... are well able to look after themselves' (Rees, 1991 p.144). Ethical questions may arise at any stage in an enquiry, but I was clear that the children's views would be a focus of this enquiry.

69

The aim of the research was to evaluate how effective the unit at Limeleigh school was, in meeting the needs of its pupils, particularly in relation to integration. A principal aim of the research was to ensure that the children themselves had a central role in that evaluation.

Data Gathering

Although initiation of the research arose from instrumental motives on the part of the headteacher, it was the head of unit who facilitated access. At no time did I need to seek permission or negotiate access to any setting. This enabled me to observe lessons and break times in all parts of the school and unit as well as interview staff and pupils. I was also given full access to children's records and other relevant LEA, school and unit documents, including policy and working papers. I attended staff meetings and met with teachers at break and dinner times: I taught some of the time and generally joined in with the everyday activities of staff and pupils. The main source of recording was open ended, with written memos of 'incidents, impressions or issues that, at the time, appeared to be significant' (Pollard and Tann, 1989 p. 31).

In this study general observations and conversational recordings were made of five unit staff, twenty two unit children, twenty mainstream staff, representatives of five support agencies (including LEA officers and police) and eighteen mainstream pupils. Individual interviews took place with all unit staff, nine key mainstream staff from a range of departments as well as the headteacher and members of the senior management team. Eight unit pupils were shadowed throughout their school day and interviewed individually as well as of part of group interviews. Nine mainstream pupils were interviewed, some of whom had specific sessions in the unit as 'non-exam' pupils.

The importance of listening to pupils

The main focus of the research was on participants' views of the role and functioning of the unit. However, I was particularly interested in the understandings which children had of their schooling. Policies and practice in education have largely developed in a top down fashion; policy makers, teachers, parents, and researchers among others, have made decisions about what is best for pupils. Children have had little opportunity to voice their opinions and have been largely disenfranchised from decision-making about their education. The children who are most vulnerable in this respect are those with 'special needs', whose relationship with the system has tended to be subordinate. However, advice emanating from the 1993 Education Act will inevitably challenge this situation. Under the Code of Practice on the Identification and Assessment of Special Educational Needs (DFE, 1994), schools are required, at certain stages in the procedure, to collect evidence about pupils' personal perceptions of their needs and how they would like to deal with them. This marks an important development in the legislation governing pupils' educational experiences and will enable pupils, for the first time in law, to take a more active role in debates about their schooling. The findings contained in this chapter reinforce the importance of listening to pupils, particularly those with complex needs.

Giving pupils, unused to such rights of expression, 'a voice' is problematic. According to HMI (1990), in its review of language and literacy, only half of the children surveyed at the age of eleven could argue a point convincingly. Children with 'special needs' are amongst those whose language skills are likely to be least developed and who are most at risk of being unable to articulate their needs, ideas and points of view (Bloom and Lahey, 1978). Recent research has highlighted the complex nature of facilitating pupil participation. For example Sinclair (1992), having reviewed the effect on services of the Children Act, 1989, concluded that; 'Increased consultation with young people and their attendance at planning meetings has still to be matched by the skills to ensure genuine participation' (p.18).

Recent work, which has looked at the issue of information exchange with pupils with 'special needs', has examined the methodological issues which underpin pupil participation in evaluations of provision. Wade and Moore (1994), in their research with pupils with a range of 'special needs', used a flexible stimulus and response format from questionnaire/structured interview and sentence-completion methods, to individual tape recordings, group discussions and children's written responses. They suggest that children choose the place where they are interviewed and dictate the pace of sessions. Minkes et al (1994) endorse this flexible approach and describe the use of pictorial and photographic aids as question prompts. They also suggest that interviews be conducted by someone well known to the child, but not directly involved with the particular service, to encourage frankness. They emphasise that care needs to be taken not to lead the child and that careful listening and observation of non-verbal responses, may prove to be revealing.

After a few weeks into the study at Limeleigh school, when the children and staff had got to know me better, I gave semi-structured interviews to pupils and staff in mainschool and unit. Throughout the study I engaged with children in groups, putting questions to them about issues which were emerging as important to them. While participation was voluntary and I attempted to avoid intruding unduly on their world, I was perceived as a member of staff. This raises questions about how voluntarily pupils engaged in this information exchange. The impression I had was that group discussions were most naturalistic, but that individual interviews were perceived as 'just another piece of schoolwork', as Denscombe and Aubrook (1992) found.

Limeleigh school

Limeleigh school has an anti-racist, multi-cultural education policy. The prospectus states that the school endeavours to promote equality of opportunity for all pupils and strongly reflects LEA policy. It goes on to describe how teaching is organised to meet the needs of children of all abilities, the academically able as well as those with learning difficulties, so that all who need it receive specialist attention. In any given academic year, approximately a quarter of pupils have reading difficulties. Out of 90 Year 7 pupils, 17% are described as two years behind in reading and 9% of pupils 4 years behind. It is estimated that 120 pupils, out of a total of 480 pupils in the school, have difficulties with literacy. There is, however one 'remedial' specialist who is designated to support all pupils. This teacher operates withdrawal classes for Year 7 'remedials' and Year 10 and 11 'non attainers'.

By using withdrawal as a means of support, and labelling pupils 'remedial' and 'non-attainers', the institution is promoting a stratified system of education. Given the deployment of resources, withdrawal was considered the most expedient system for special needs support. However some pupils become marginalised from everyday educational experiences, and by application of a system of negative labelling children run the risk of becoming alienated (Hargreaves, 1967). For some pupils at Limeleigh this meant they ended up joining pupils from the unit for lessons; thus, as will be discussed later, mainstream 'remedials' are relegated to the lowest status group in the school.

The Unit

It is in a school with a relatively high proportion of pupils with special needs and with limited means for effective support, that the unit was located. LEA policy was to position units in mainstream to integrate mainschool and unit pupils. Limeleigh unit consists of a series of inter-linking classrooms in one of the main teaching blocks. School documentation describes it as a 'special unit' which is staffed by 'specialist teachers' trained to meet the needs of 'statemented pupils'. These children are 'supervised' in 'their own accommodation'. The discourse in which these descriptions are embedded signals 'otherness', important differences and a separate agenda from the rest. Unit pupils are described as 'statemented'; they are 'supervised', not taught, as would be expected of school aged children; they spend their time with 'specialist' not everyday teachers in 'separate' accommodation. This description eschews a concern to elucidate similarities and needs shared with other pupils; it signals a separate, segregationist agenda which is at odds with LEA integrationist policies.

Pupils at Limeleigh Unit

There were twenty-two pupils on roll in the unit at Limeleigh school at the time of the study. Of these 18 (82%) were described in teachers' records as having emotional and behavioural difficulties. The majority had 'acting out' difficulties where they were described as aggressive to family members as well as to teachers and peers. Three pupils were described as having self-damaging behaviour. Thirteen pupils (65%) experienced difficulties in reading, writing and spelling; for five pupils this was due to language disorder or delay and for two pupils this was linked to English being their second language. Twenty pupils (90%) were statemented under provisions of the 1981 (now 1993) Education Act, and the remaining two pupils were awaiting statements while being assessed at the unit. All statements recommended 'highly structured teaching programmes', only four suggested pupils would benefit from mainstream curriculum with support. While teachers' records identified eighteen pupils as having predominantly emotional and behavioural difficulties, only five of the twenty statements came to this conclusion. These statements specified that pupils receive counselling in social and coping strategies in two cases, firm discipline in one, and home-school liaison to ensure continuity of behaviour management, for another two pupils. The majority of statements emphasised individualised curricular programmes while teachers' records focused on the primary importance of behaviour management. This has important implications for provision in relation to integration where there is an obvious tension between needs as perceived by the authors of the statements, and the teachers.

Also, given that the LEA endorses integration and the unit is located in the heart of a comprehensive school, it is surprising that only four of the twenty statements referred to pupils benefiting from integration. While two pupils from the unit spent 80% of their time in mainschool lessons with mainstream pupils, the remainder spent most of their integrated experience in mainschool classes being taught by comprehensive school staff with other unit pupils, not mainstream children. Interpretations of what is meant by 'integration' clearly vary.

Research findings

Pupil perceptions about the role of the unit

The perceptions of the role of the unit are first reflected in how unit pupils thought mainstream children viewed and described them. Descriptions were wholly pejorative. The term 'unit kid' had become a new form of negative labelling to be added to the more usual terms. Data were obtained from observations and conversational recordings with pupils in groups as well as through individual interviews.

(The codes at the end of quotations refer to whether pupils are unit pupils (U.P.) or mainschool pupils (MP) and their year group and gender.)

> Other kids say the unit's a dunce's place for stupid kids who act silly. UP. Yr. 9. (F)

> They call you stupid kids, are you having your lessons over there then? They think you're dossing. UP. Yr. 10. (M)

> Other kids say the unit is for dunce people and spastics who ain't got much sense. UP. Yr. 11. (M)

> They (mainschool) call us unit kids and provoke us and say we are spastics. He look like one himself. (Jabbing fingers toward mainschool boy). UP. Yr. 11. (F)

> Mainschool kids tease you, they see the unit as a place for mental people — less better than themselves. UP. Yr. 8. (M)

Unit pupils were fully cognisant of the names mainschool pupils called them and aware that this meant they were perceived as inferior in both their capacity to learn and to behave. The use of pejorative labels about unit pupils' inherent qualities and abilities denotes the discriminatory attitudes of mainschool pupils. This in itself, it can be argued, has profound implications for pupils placed in this unit. Unit pupils were aware that they had become an identified category of children with inferior credentials, with a lower status than the rest.

Labelling theory offers one a way of understanding the processes in play in Limeleigh school and the implications of being labelled a 'unit kid'. Becker (1963), one of the originators of the theory, argued that deviance is created by societies, such as schools, attaching negative labels to those who are regarded as committing deviant acts. He argues that these labels may be assigned because of stereotyped perceptions held by others in those environments. These assumptions are frequently derived from stereotypical images and perceptions based on social class, ethnic origin and gender.

Hargreaves (1975) described how labelling influences the self-concept of pupils such that they become engulfed by that label and a cycle of events is in place whereby the labelled pupil is isolated, excluded and treated differently, for example placed in a special unit with other 'problem' pupils. When the pupil reacts with hostility and frustration to these restrictions, this is deemed to be proof of the trustworthiness of the original label.

The results of this process are that children who have negative labels attached to them suffer some degree of isolation, identify with those similarly labelled and reject the standards and mores of the majority (Corrigan, 1979, Burgess, 1983). Evidence from this study shows that a negative cycle of events was reinforced by children being assigned unit placements. The negative stereotyping of unit pupils was partially due to mainstream pupils' attitudes being transmitted to them. For the most part unit children described how they were perceived in the eyes of mainschool children, not teachers. What was striking was how consonant the descriptions were between groups. Also significant was the distance which mainschool children put between themselves and unit pupils. The latter, thus labelled, suffer marginalisation, not only due to their closing ranks, but due to mainstream pupils distancing themselves. This is demonstrated in a representative sample of comments expressed by mainstream pupils:

I don't bother them and they don't bother me. MP. Yr.9, (M)

It's nothing to do with me what they do. MP. Yr.9, (M)

Unit pupils are seen as strange, not part of the community. MP Yr.11, (F)

They try to act normal, but they're not treated normal. MP. Yr.11, (F)

Of the eighteen mainstream pupils I spoke with, none spoke positively about the unit or its pupils, the least negative responses were those of disinterest; the majority were pejorative.

It's for spastics up there. What's it got to do with us? MP. Yr.9, (M)

It's for dossers up there, I don't even notice them in the playground. MP. Yr.9, (M)

The Unit's a dunces' hole. The kids are in it because they act silly. I've got my own friends. MP. Yr.10, (M)

The categorisation and marginalisation of pupils on the grounds of their abilities to conform to 'normal' educational and behavioural standards is a formative influence on the experience of education at Limeleigh school. Being a member of the unit relegated pupils to a stigmatised, inferior and marginal status. Unit pupils identified with the unit subculture. The focus of their identification however was not generally with fellow pupils but with unit teachers.

Pupils' views of unit staff

Unit pupils generally expressed positive attitudes towards unit teachers. One pupil, who was very isolated, with profound social problems, had a positive view of unit staff.

> I don't like being with people, I don't like other kids. I've got no best friends, no friends at all. Other kids don't like me, but I do like my teachers (in the unit). UP. Yr.11, (M)

Such positive comments about unit teachers were generally juxtaposed with negative comments about mainstream staff. Unit staff were perceived as providing a safe place, a sanctuary where pupils could feel relatively relaxed. Being in mainschool was generally depicted as negative, though one girl did admit to having a positive experience in mainschool, receiving a merit for work well done.

> I think the unit teachers do a good job, I feel more relaxed with these teachers. Mainschool teachers are horribler than unit ones, but I got a merit for a letter rack (in mainschool). UP. Yr.11, (F)

While unit staff were described as 'nice, kind and loose', one pupil perceived the unit's safety in terms of a unit teacher's ability to control pupils.

> Some teachers in mainschool think they're really hard — tough nuts. Teachers in the unit are a little bit loose and don't mind if you're a little bit late. I'm up here for tempers and fighting, they suspend and expel you for tempers in mainschool. C he had bad problems. Teacher (from unit) came in and he calms him down. UP. Yr.9, (F)

The image of the unit being perceived as safe and yet a place where children could be 'sorted out' was referred to repeatedly. The perception of mainschool as a hostile environment also featured strongly.

> Here you have jokes and everything. Teacher shouts a lot, nice when he want to be, but he can be a pain. Once I got beaten up by a mainschool 3rd year in a queue for tuck shop. Come to unit crying and explain it all to teacher. He sort him out. People I love most are N (U.P. Yr.11) and all unit teachers. UP. Yr.11, (F)

> I like unit staff because they're nice and kind. If you didn't have a unit you'd be in mainschool all the time and that would be terrible, lousy and boring, the other kids would be nasty. Units are good because you feel safer here. UP. Yr.10, (F)

> I like the unit better than my last school. At my other school I was always in the same class, it was boring, especially if you had a rotten teacher. In the unit I feel liked, the teachers are really nice, all of them. In mainschool they ain't got much time for you and shout and every-

thing at you. Now I'm better behaved I've got more friends, but in the unit some kids are badly behaved though. UP. Yr.9, (M)

The unit staff do a good job. I feel more relaxed with these staff. Mainschool staff are OK but lose tempers a lot and go on at you, a bit too strict really. UP. Yr.9, (M)

Mainschool teachers think the unit is stupid so they don't take much notice of you. UP. Yr.8, (M)

Unit teachers here have got time and patience to help. If you've got problems you can talk to them. UP. Yr.8, (M)

All of these pupils had been labelled at some point as unsuited to ordinary, mainstream education. Their statements and subsequent unit placements were confirmation of this. These children had shared histories of displacement from ordinary schools. That they perceived mainschool teachers as hostile was therefore understandable, also, the fact that the unit was regarded as a safe place was of profound importance. The role of the unit in the eyes of the children was to provide a preferred alternative to mainschool where teachers were likely to be short tempered, hard or 'tough nuts'. Unit teachers were generally liked by unit children not only because they were 'loose, kind and patient', but because they could paradoxically 'sort people out' when necessary. These views reinforce the notion that the unit was perceived as a sanctuary by its pupils, not a means of accessing mainschool.

Unit pupil perceptions of integration

A major justification for the unit at Limeleigh according to LEA and school policies was that it facilitated the integration of pupils with special needs and provided opportunities for social interaction between mainschool and unit pupils. However, when pupils from the unit talk about their participation in mainstream life, a different picture emerges.

Mainschool kids say horrible things about the unit. I stay away from them as much as I can. UP. Yr. 9, (F)

I don't bother with friends in the playground, just stand there. Break soon ends, it's only twenty minutes. UP. Yr.11, (M)

I get bullied sometimes, W. (mainstream boy) tries to trip me up. I wish I didn't have to go out. UP. Yr.11, (F)

I don't like the playground. I would rather be somewhere else. I don't like the unit much, I would rather be in another secondary school. I wouldn't want to be in mainschool for lessons though, I hate the big school. UP. Yr10, (M)

The playground's too big. I've got no one to play with. I'd like to be at home with Mum and Dad. UP. Yr.9, (M)

These quotations were representative of the attitudes of the majority of unit pupils and borne out by observations made using time sampling with the Parten (1932-33) categories of social participation. Four of the eight pupils observed, over two weeks, at break and dinner times, were solitary. Three of the remaining pupils played with other children from the unit, and one year eleven girl played, for the most part, with two Year 7 mainschool pupils. Two of the solitary pupils avoided social contact by either moving away when anyone came within ten feet or by avoiding eye contact. The pupils who played together tended to stay near to adults on duty and frequently approached them to tell them pupils were picking on them by calling them names, kicking them or even looking at them.

Much has been written about the negative effects of streaming on pupils' self-esteem and informal social relationships (Hargreaves, 1967, Lacey, 1970, Corrigan, 1979). Corrigan noted how pupils can become alienated by being in marginal groups in the school (lower streams), while Hargreaves showed how behaviour difficulties among pupils are more strongly associated with school organisation than within-child characteristics. These writers make a direct link between school organisation, pupil self-esteem and educational progress and social acceptability or integration.

The unit in this study is effectively more segregated than a lower stream. It has a separate label and identity which is linked with children being seen as different and inferior. In turn this means that social stratification takes place in the playground, children from mainstream and unit fail to mix. Rather than the playground reducing stigmatisation and giving unit children a sense of being mainstream, it confirms their differences and acts as a constant reminder of their perceived inferiority and deficit labels. This evidence supports the contention that labelling leads to stereotyping and marginalisation. Further, it suggests wider implications of this particular form of educational practice as there is evidence from this study that further distress is experienced by pupils, who are already under pressure, by their daily exposure to these playground experiences. Their distress results from educational policies and school practices which were designed to have the opposite effect.

Integration in mainstream lessons

The other arena for social contact of unit and mainstream pupils was in ordinary lessons. Most pupils had mainschool experiences in half way classes, where a mainschool teacher taught a group of unit pupils. Two pupils, who had three lessons per week with mainschool children, were tracked. The following comments are from these two pupils.

> I'm not doing an exam in mainschool. Don't do what the other kids do, sometimes my reading, spelling and writing not all that good. Get exhausted, wears you out. I would rather be in the unit all the time. UP. Yr.10, (F)

> Sometimes in mainschool I find things hard to understand. I'm afraid to ask for help because I feel shy, but I try to hide it. I don't like going across for lessons much. UP. Yr.11, (M)

The pedagogic and social isolation of 'integrated' unit pupils which these comments depict was reinforced by the observations carried out in the school. While these children were physically located in a mainschool classroom, they sat and worked alone. In contrast two statemented pupils who had more than 80% of their timetables in fully integrated lessons spoke positively about mainschool (these pupils were on the registers of mainstream classes):

> I've got lots of friends, one friend who's in the unit, all the others are in the mainschool. I got friendly in the classroom, just started to sit by them and got friends. UP. Yr.10, (M)

> I've got no best friend, but I've got friends, mainly in the mainschool. They are mostly in my form (for registration). UP. Yr.10, (M)

One explanation for these pupils being able to integrate more successfully might be that they were more able academically and had greater social skills. And yet both had originally been statemented and put into the unit because of their learning and behaviour difficulties. Therefore another explanation might be that they were less stigmatised because they had a common base of shared educational experiences. It has been argued that the most effective way of helping vulnerable pupils is to implement an integrated, mixed ability teaching approach as advocated by Kyriacou (1986) and Sayer (1987). In this way children are less likely to suffer the negative labelling and alienation which comes from being segregated from their peer group. These writers also argue that by ensuring all children remain the responsibility of their subject teachers, staff gain the professional competence and confidence to cope effectively with a wide range of pupils.

Unit pupils' perceptions of teaching/learning in mainstream and unit

Pupils' attitudes toward where they preferred to be taught reflected implicit understandings about the unit being a stigmatised learning environment. They were conscious of the fact that it was a place where pupils were perceived as 'not brainy', 'spastics' or 'dossers'. On a one to one basis pupils were much more openly supportive and appreciative of what the unit offered; equally they were more negative and critical of mainstream. In group situations however, pupils were more guarded, they appeared to feel stigmatised about admitting the need for help and would frequently speak in the third person about the benefits of unit teaching often prefacing comments about the unit by expressing the desire to be in mainstream.

> I would rather be in mainschool, but the unit is a place where people can get extra help. UP. Yr.8, (M)

> I would rather be in mainschool lessons, but the unit's a good idea for people who can't read. UP. Yr. 10, (M)

> I would rather be in ordinary lessons, but they do phonics here to help if you need it. UP. Yr.8, (M)

> It's good for people who are deaf and E2L problems, but I would rather be in mainschool all the time. It's not too bad in classes. UP. Yr.10, (M)

> I failed English so I come up for some peace and quiet, so I can concentrate on other subjects, comprehension and maths. I used to feel a stigma about coming here, now people look up to me, I don't worry about coming here. MP Yr.11, (M)

> I'm up here for tempers and fighting, not work, some of us know what we're doing with our work. UP. Yr.9, (F)

Two themes developed in group sessions. Firstly, that the unit provided appropriate help for people who needed extra curriculum support, though no pupil admitted in such sessions that they needed this kind of help. Secondly, it was acceptable to admit in front of other pupils that you were in the unit for bad behaviour but not for an inability to keep up with work. Most pupils in the group sessions agreed that they preferred to be in mainschool 'because you get proper lessons there' (U.P. Yr.10, (M).) However, when pupils were interviewed on their own a different picture emerged, one where the unit was perceived as providing help when pupils got stuck and which was undoubtedly the preferred alternative to mainschool.

> The unit teachers teach you good things, I get a good education in the unit and everything. If you left school now the unit helps you to get a job, I get good help here. UP. Yr.11, (F)

> In the unit I do a lot of reading and all this. Teachers spend more time with you, my mum is well pleased with my progress. U.P., Yr.9, (M)

> They use the phonic blend system and you get more attention than in the main school. UP. Yr.8, (M)

Publicly the children reflected the dominant school culture in their attitudes to academic achievement. They perceived failure in this arena as something from which to disassociate themselves. While acknowledging that the unit offered good support for other pupils, the criterion they used to admit their own association with the unit was on the grounds of tempers and fighting. Publicly children expressed the desire to be in mainschool for their lessons, privately they admitted to disliking their lessons, finding it difficult to keep up and understand. The pressure to appear to be able to do the same as mainstream children was in evidence: but a private acknowledgement that it was preferable to be helped in the unit showed insight into their own difficulties.

Discussion

This study revealed a disjunction between policy and practice. Other examples are given in the literature. For example, Troyna (1993) who scrutinises 'the enduring discrepancies between rhetoric and practice' in relation to antiracist and multicultural education policies (p.43). In the case of the Limeleigh study, the disjunction is between official integrationist policy, in which a unit for statemented children is located centrally in a school with a commitment to equal opportunities for all its pupils, and the actual social and psychological marginalisation of the 'special' pupils. The rift is tacitly acknowledged in the language of the school's own documentation which describes pupils from the unit as 'statemented' and 'supervised' in 'separate' accommodation by 'specialist' teachers. This discourse fails to demonstrate similarities and shared needs with mainschool counterparts; rather it communicates differences. The inspection reports referred to earlier also noted the isolation of unit pupils in both social and curricular terms. The head of the school recognised this problem and had tried to implement a number of strategies to change the situation, including inviting me in. But segregationist practice was deeply embedded in, and sustained by, the culture of the school. Staff persisted in defining unit pupils as having emotional and behavioural difficulties when their statements did not identify such difficulties as dominant. Provision to meet the needs of these pupils was based on conflicting perceptions of its purpose by local authority and teaching staff. This has major implications for integration in practice.

Pupils presented a picture at Limeleigh in which there was a deep division between two categories of pupils. It is through the words of the children that these divisions are most graphically revealed. Their awareness of their image among peers and of their low status in the pupil subculture tells us more about policy than official descriptions. A stark picture emerged of breaktime being an experience to endure. Some unit pupils distanced themselves from mainschool pupils and even other unit pupils, an isolation born of mistrust and fear. For some pupils from the unit the only people they really liked were unit teachers. What are the implications of this for school policy? Was the policy out of touch with pupils' needs? One explanation relates to the fact that the key participants in this situation, the children and teachers, have had little involvement in policy construction. Staff subconsciously, or consciously, subvert attempts to harmonise practice between mainschool and unit. This may be due to their close contact with unit pupils. While it was never articulated by staff, there was an implicit understanding that the children themselves identify first and foremost with the unit. This 'loyalty' is tacitly reinforced by teachers in the unit.

Pupils' comments reveal that they did not want to cross the rigidly defined boundaries between mainschool and unit. Apart from the two boys who were integrated for most of the time, pupils from the unit failed to mix with those from mainstream; they were psychologically unit-bound. This raises questions about integration in action, about the monitoring of effectiveness and evaluating the outcomes of educational initiatives. Children from the unit saw it as a sanctuary, a safe place away from the stresses of mainschool. Integration was not something they aspired to, on the contrary they generally endured their contacts with mainstream, both in the classroom and the playground. The unit therefore failed in its primary aim to facilitate integration, it acted as a mechanism which promoted segregation. In this sense, paradoxically, it might be argued it met the needs of its pupils.

This research reports one set of findings which may not be generalisable to other situations. However what it can do as a case study, according to Elliot (1990), is paint an empirical picture and a provisional theoretical explanation of events for others to consider in their own context and through which they can examine their own practice. The dominant message which emerged from this study was that by listening to the children, integration could be shown to be failing, despite a widespread assumption among those responsible for it that it was effective. Evaluation of policy and practice needs to place pupils centre stage, if education is to develop responsively.

References

Ball, S. (1984) Beachside Reconsidered: Reflections on a Methodological Apprenticeship in Burgess R.G. *The Research Process in Educational Settings: Ten Case Studies*, London: The Falmer Press.

Becker, H. (1963) *Outsiders*, Oxford, Free Press.

Bell, J. (1987) *Doing Your Research Project*, Milton Keynes: Open University Press.

Bloom, L. and Lahey, M. (1978) *Language Development and Language Disorders*, New York: Wiley Inc.

Bulmer, M. (1980) Comments on the ethics of covert methods, *British Journal of Sociology*, 31(1) pp 59-65.

Burgess, R. (1983) *Experiencing Comprehensive Education*, London: Methuen.

Corrigan, P. (1979) *Schooling the Smash Street Kids*, London: Macmillan Press.

Davies, J. and West, A. (1985) The Reintegration of Pupils into Mainstream Schools. *Research and Statistics*, ILEA.

Denscombe, M. and Aubrook, L. (1992) 'It's just another peice of school work': the ethics of questionnaire research on pupils in schools. *British Education Research Journal*, 18, 2:92 pp.113-131.

DES (1978a) *Special Educational Needs. Report of the Committee of Enquiry into the Education of Handicapped Children and Young People, (The Warnock Report)* London, HMSO.

DES (1978b) *Behavioural Units. A Survey of Special Units of Pupils with Behavioural Problems*, London, HMSO.

DFE (1993) *Pupils with Problems, the Education by LEAs of children otherwise than at school*, Circular 4, London, DFE.

DFE (1994) *Code of Practice on the Identification and Assessment of Special Educational Needs*, London, DFE.

Elliot, J. (1990) 'Validating Case Studies', *Westminster Studies in Education*, 13. pp 47-60.

Gallie, W.B. (1955-56) Essentially contested concepts, *Proceedings of the Aristotelian Society*, 56, pp.167-198.

Hammersley, M. (ed.) (1986) *Controversies in Classroom Research,* Milton Keynes: Open University Press.

Hargreaves, D.H. (1967) *Social Relationships in a Secondary School.* London, Routledge and Kegan Paul.

Hargreaves, D. (1984) *Improving Secondary Schools, Report of the Committee on the Curriculum and Organisation of Secondary Schools.* London, ILEA.

HMI (1990) *Aspects of Primary Education: The Teaching and Learning of Language and Literacy*, London, HMSO.

Hurford, A. and Hart, D. (1979) Social Integration in a Language Unit. *Special Education*, Vol. 6, No.4. pp 8-10.

Kyriacou, C. (1986) *Effective Teaching in Schools*, Oxford: Blackwell.

Lacey, C. (1970) *Hightown Grammar.* Manchester: Manchester University Press.

Lowden, G. (1985) The Units Approach to Integration. *British Journal of Special Education.* Vol.12 , No.1. pp.10-12.

Minkes, J., Robinson, C. and Weston, C. (1994) 'Consulting the Children: interviews with children using residential respite care services', *Disability and Society*, Vol.9, No.1. pp. 47-57.

OFSTED (1993) *Education for Disaffected Pupils*, Ref 1/93/NS. London, DFE.

Parten, M.B. (1932-33) Social participation among pre-school children *Journal of Abnormal and Social Psychology* 27, pp.243-269.

Pollard, A. and Tann, S. (1989) *Reflective Teaching in the Primary School*, London, Cassell.

Rees, T. (1991) Ethical Issues in Allan, G. and Skinner, C. L. (eds) *Handbook for Research Students in the Social Sciences*, London: Falmer.

Sayer, J. (1987) *Special Needs in the Ordinary School*, London: Cassell.

Sinclair, R. (1992) Happy Birthday, Children Act, *Community Care 1* October 1992.

Troyna, B. (1993) *Racism and Education: Research Perspectives*, Buckingham: Open University Press.

Wade, B. and Moore, M. (1992) *Patterns of Educational Integration. International Perspectives on Mainstreaming Children with Special Educational Needs*, Wallingford, Triangle Books Ltd.

Wade, B. and Moore, M. (1994) Good for a Change? The Views of Students with Special Educational Needs on Changing School, *Pastoral Care* 12(2), pp.23-27.

Chapter 6

When Segregation Works:
Pupils' Experience of Residential Special Provision

Paul W. Cooper

Introduction

This chapter is a personal account of a research study into the effects of residential schooling. At the time of the study I was a teacher in a residential school for boys with emotional and behavioural difficulties (EBD), having spent three years as an English teacher in a comprehensive school.

The years I spent in the latter school were as brutal an experience to me as I believe they were to many of the pupils who went there. From the barbed wire over the gates, to the dingy quarry floor, painted brick and white tiles of the corridors, to the brain drilling bells. And yet this was not a bad school, in the way that schools can sometimes be bad. Staff-room cynicism was tempered by a general and genuine concern for pupils' learning and welfare. There was always, however, a sense of helplessness: the feeling that there was not an awful lot that could be done to cater effectively for many of our pupils' needs. The problems that the pupils brought with them from their home backgrounds, the appalling lack of adequate resources and accommodation in the school, and the increasingly hostile and confrontational political climate all seemed just too much.

Since then I have taught in a number of different settings: as a peripatetic teacher for children with EBD; in a residential school for boys with EBD; in a mainstream junior school; in an off-site unit for secondary school children with adjustment problems. Since 1988 I have worked in higher education, as an educational researcher and lecturer. This chapter contains some of the ideas that I have come to value, that I think would have been useful to my colleagues in the comprehensive school, and might have helped them to feel less helpless and overwhelmed.

The chapter is largely based on a detailed study of 77 boys' perceptions of the experience and effects of residential schooling. It was carried out in two residential schools for boys with EBD. Two opening sections, deal with (1) why we should concern ourselves with residential pupils' perspectives of their circumstances, and (2) how I went about accessing these perspectives.

Disclaimer

This chapter is not intended to suggest that the segregation of pupils with EBD is always the desirable alternative to mainstream integration or 'inclusive' education for such children. The chapter is about the way in which the residential option was often a positive experience for a group of children, and can sometimes be a 'positive choice' for other children, as the authors of the 1988 Wagner Report suggest. The chapter is also about some of the aspects of residential provision that might inform practice in mainstream schools and so strengthen the likelihood of preventive and integrational strategies working in these settings. An important subtext here is that it is dangerous and unhelpful to be dogmatic about integration and segregation. The important thing is informed choice: to choose the option that best fits the needs and circumstances that are involved in each case.

Background

Such a study was necessary for the following reasons:

1. Residential schools for children with emotional and behavioural difficulties (EBD) have been neglected in recent years by educational researchers. Even more neglected is the study of pupils' perceptions of the residential experience. Dawson (1984) is an exception to this, in that he provides systematic data on pupils' contemporaneous perceptions of their experience of residential (EBD) schooling. A more recent exception is provided by Grimshaw and Berridge (1994). Their in-depth study of residential schools shares many common features and conclusions with earlier accounts of the research presented here (see Cooper 1989, 1992, 1993a, 1993b, 1993c, Cooper, Smith and Upton, 1994).

2. Residential schools have for some time been seen increasingly as a last resort: 'a pragmatic second best' (Cole, 1986). This view, which is reflected in low staff morale, is often expressed without reference to concrete research evidence about what actually happens in residential schools and how they affect the lives of their pupils, or is based on worst-case examples. Residential schools are also sometimes condemned by association with custodial institutions for delinquents (e.g. Millham, Bullock and Cherrett, 1975; Millham, Bullock and Hosie, 1978).

3. Uncritical integrationist dogma tends to ignore the effects of bad mainstream schools. Whilst integration may be desirable, is it always possible? When we come to consider the practical realities of integration, we have to recognise that some schools are simply unfit places for vulnerable children.

The current study was partly inspired by the wealth of literature by pioneer practitioners in residential education for children with EBD (discussed below), which makes claims as to the positive effects of this form of provision on children with EBD. Important questions suggested by this were:

> to what extent would these claims stand up to systematic scrutiny by an impartial researcher?

if the claims were in any way substantiated, what implications might they have for mainstream schools, and so contribute to our understanding of school effectiveness?

4. There is a pool of published writing and research from the social work field which takes a more balanced view of the integration question (Davis, 1981; Potter, 1986). Here residential care has been portrayed by some as a positive option in certain circumstances because it offers the possibility of supplementing and complementing family care, rather than replacing and undermining family solidarity with foster families. The Wagner Report (1988) argues this case forcefully, emphasising the need for a continuum of care which includes both community based and residential options, with the possibility of free movement between the various stages on the continuum.

5. There are interesting conceptual links between school and teacher effectiveness research (e.g. Rutter et al., 1979; Reynolds and Sullivan, 1979; Reynolds, 1976, 1984; Purkey and Smith, 1983; Mortimore et al., 1988) and the writings of the pioneer residential workers with EBD children, such as Neill (1916 ,1968), Wills (1960), Lyward (Burn, 1956), Shaw (1956, 1969), Balbernie (1966), Bettelheim (1950, 1955), and Lennhoff (1966); see Bridgeland (1971). These pioneers stressed the importance of good quality staff-pupil relationships, the value of pupil participation and 'shared responsibility', the need for a responsive school environment and the importance of therapeutic rather than coercive responses to behavioural problems.

School effectiveness research is pointing out the important role these (and other) ideas play in effective mainstream schools. Also, the emphasis on good quality relationships, pupil needs, and opportunities for involvement in school life stand in direct opposition to the 'institutionalisation' arguments noted above. The pioneers were in fact among the first to advocate the importance of these values in educational contexts, and were putting these ideas into practice long before they had even gained acceptance among teachers in mainstream schools. The pioneers often complained about the dehumanising and destructive effects of mainstream schools, to which they claimed to offer a positive alternative. Dawson (1981) suggests that some of the central concepts professed by the pioneers are detectable in modern residential school practice, a point which further undermines the blanket 'institutionalisation' argument, which suggests that residential schooling is damaging and undesirable, *per se.*

Taken together these issues leave us with a great many unanswered questions about residential schools for pupils with EBD. This study, therefore, set out to answer some of these questions, the main ones being:

1. What are the effects of residential schooling on pupils with EBD?

2. What patterns of organisational features exist in such schools?

3. How might staff-inmate relationships be best characterised in such schools?

4. What forms of inmate adaptation do such schools engender?

5. To what extent, if any, does the residential school experience contribute to the resolution of pupils' perceived emotional and behavioural difficulties?

The Study

In order to answer these questions, the 'grounded' approach was adopted (Glaser and Strauss, 1968). This approach seeks to develop theory out of data, rather than collecting data in order to test theories. The ethnographic case-study method is most commonly associated with this approach, its intention being to gather data which describe the perceptions and behaviour patterns of participants in the research setting. The analysis of the data is intended to uncover theories which are implicit in the everyday actions and activities of the participants.

The concern with grounded theory was of central importance because there was so little existing research on which to base hypotheses about the possible nature and effects of residential schooling on EBD pupils. Although the research sought answers to specific questions relating to modes of pupils' adaptation and institutional arrangements, it was necessary to recognise that answers to these questions may not be of central significance in the final analysis. The adoption of an open-ended, 'grounded' approach was therefore an appropriate means of allowing information about teachers' and pupils' central concerns to come to the fore.

A further consideration which made the grounded approach appropriate is the central significance that is attributed to pupil perceptions in this research. This approach derives from the view that any understanding of how human behaviour relates to experience must take account of the ways in which the experience is perceived by actors, since human beings behave in accordance with the ways in which they interpret their experience. This view has particular resonance for those interested in behavioural problems, recognising as it does the distinctions that need to be made between the knowledge that can be gained from the individuals' first-hand account of their own behaviour and that which can be gained from observation alone. To understand the ways in which schools, teachers and classrooms influence pupil behaviour we must explore the mediating effects of pupil cognitions (Wittrock, 1986) and analyse the meanings they attach to everyday events (Woods, 1990; Cronk, 1987; Schostak, 1983; Willis, 1978; Tattum, 1982; Rosser and Harré, 1976).

Method

Two residential EBD schools for secondary school-aged boys were selected for the study. This gave a basis for comparison between schools, whilst maintaining a manageable number of participants and opportunities to develop a detailed knowledge of each school. The two schools adhered to a broadly similar pattern, though having interesting individual and apparently contrasting features. Considerations of accessibility and willingness to participate were prime considerations in the choice of schools. Both were independently operated, although fees came from public sources, and they were located in rural surroundings. There were 32 pupils on roll at Lakeside and 45 on roll at Farfield. Pupils were referred to both schools solely by local education authorities. Farfield school charged considerably higher fees than Lakeside (double, on average), though Farfield took some pupils on 52-week placements, whilst Lakeside only catered for pupils during term time. The officially espoused policies of both schools were to adopt a 'therapeutic' approach.

In many ways Lakeside had more of an 'institutional' feel about it, with few of the obvious home comforts in evidence at Farfield. In fact, the economic disparities between the two schools were clearly evident on a superficial level. Lakeside had more the appearance of a formal school about it, with boys wearing a secondary school style uniform (grey trousers, white shirt and school tie), whilst Farfield boys wore no uniform. Yet Lakeside boys addressed the staff by their Christian names while at Farfield the usual mode of address was 'Sir' or 'Miss', or title and family name. These superficial differences suggested possible deeper points of contrast that it was felt would repay research.

Data collection methods included:

Participant and non-participant observation
Tape-recorded interviews
Self-completed questionnaires
Document analysis.

Reflexivity

A key principle which should underpin all ethnographic studies of this kind is that of 'reflexivity' (Hammersley and Atkinson, 1983). 'Reflexivity' refers to the researcher's need to maintain an awareness of the effect that he or she is having on the situation which he or she is studying. This involves paying careful attention to the way in which the researchers present themselves to their subjects, the kinds of relationships ('field relations') they develop with subjects, the indications they receive as to how they are perceived by subjects, and methods that researchers employ to motivate subjects to co-operate.

Reflexivity was of particular importance to this study, since I was teaching in one of the schools (Farfield), and had been for over two years. This situation forced me to consider the differences between the role of the teacher and that of the researcher, and to develop procedures which effectively communicated the researcher role. The most obvious difference (for me) between researcher and teacher was the difference in power relations that the two roles implied, and the different constraints and expectations that each role implies for both teacher-researcher and pupils. As a teacher, one is required to take a lead and to make judgements; as a researcher one adopts a non-judgemental, impartial attitude and tries to empower the subject to lead. What is common to both roles is the importance of trust in the relationship. Subjects will not reveal their beliefs and attitudes unless they have reason to believe in the integrity of the researcher. Similarly, pupils who do not trust their teachers will often withhold their co-operation (Rosser and Harré, 1976; Tattum, 1982). In retrospect, I think that the kinds of relationships that I had developed with pupils as a teacher made the transition to researcher less difficult than it might have been. I think this has something to do with the relative informality of the small residential school setting, and the emphasis, which is common in such schools, on fairly informal and co-operative relationships between staff and pupils.

Formal procedures developed to deal with the transition from the teacher to the researcher-role (at Farfield) involved:

> portraying the study to pupils as one concerned with the experience of residential schooling as they perceive it; indicating to pupils their expert status in relation to this knowledge, and describing the possible beneficial outcomes of such a study to themselves and other consumers of educational services;
>
> establishing to pupils the voluntary nature of their involvement in the study, and accepting refusals without question (only one pupil refused to be interviewed in the entire study);
>
> carrying out interviews during pupils' free time, and in my own off-duty hours;
>
> carrying out some participant observation in my own off-duty hours;
>
> asking pupils to choose a time when it would be convenient for them to be interviewed (if they chose to be);
>
> assuring pupils of the strict confidentiality of their interview data, within the realms of legality;
>
> deliberately avoiding judgmental responses during interviews;
>
> deliberately showing empathy and acceptance during interviews;
>
> deliberately avoiding references to the study during lessons/duty periods, unless the subject was raised by pupils.

The Lakeside study was less complicated than the Farfield study in that I was known to the staff and students of Lakeside as a researcher only. There were, however, other difficulties to negotiate there. The major problem, which is common to most studies of this type, was that of motivating the potential participants to co-operate. I attended the school on several occasions before I embarked on the interview programme, mixing with pupils on an informal basis and joining in with their leisure activities. As at Farfield, the boys became increasingly curious about my study and after a while I had no trouble in recruiting interviewees.

Data Gathering

Interviews were carried out with a total of 24 boys (15 from Farfield and 9 from Lakeside). These boys were all over 14 and made up the 'senior' pupil groups of both schools (only one boy in this age-group refused to be interviewed). In addition to the interviews, two questionnaires were developed for use with pupils. These questionnaires were constructed after an initial analysis of the interview data, in order to test the generalisability of some of the findings across both school populations.

Although the primary focus of the study was the pupils' perspective, interviews and questionnaires were applied to staff also. There was also a good deal of informal data gathering on the staff side; this included notes made on conversations I had with staff, and notes on staff discussions at which I was present. Teachers' opinions were also gathered about the effectiveness of the school and the perceived importance of school aims.

Interviews with both staff and pupils were intended to be of the 'informant' type, as opposed to the 'respondent' type (Powney and Watts, 1987). Pupil interviews opened with the question: 'Can you remember what you thought of this school when you first came here?' Staff interviews often began with a question such as: 'Could you tell me something about what it is like to work in this school?'

The interview then developed on the basis of the interviewee's response to this question, with the interviewer seeking elaboration and exemplification. Interviewees were encouraged to concentrate on specific experiences. When they spoke in generalised terms they were asked to provide concrete examples from their own experience. The interview procedures owed a great deal to techniques developed in counselling psychology, particularly Rogers' Person-Centred approach (Rogers', 1951; 1980). This involves the utilisation of a number of interpersonal skills designed to encourage the interviewee to feel secure, accepted, and able to disclose his or her own concerns.

Participant and non-participant observation were used essentially as an impression gathering exercise. The primary data was always the interview material. The participant observation involved mainly my engagement in leisure and hobby activities with the pupils, mealtimes, and my presence in staff-rooms during some breaks and lunch-times. Non-participant observation took place in classrooms, during lessons, in assemblies, and in school and staff meetings. Obviously, at Farfield my participation was much more that of a staff member, in addition to these other areas. The observation also provided a common experience for the interviewees and myself, which was an important source in interviews. I based no conclusions on observational data alone, only using this data when it proved of relevance to information gained in interviews. Sometimes observed events were used as a basis for interview questions. Observational data was also used to exemplify and, in some cases, qualify insights derived from interviews.

An analysis was conducted of various official documents that the schools produced for the public, in which they professed school aims. Also included were internal discussion documents, as well as pupils' reports and records. The aim of this analysis was to develop an image of the formal espoused aims and concerns of the schools, as well as their organisational structures.

The principle of progressive focusing was applied in the analysis of interview material. This involves the systematic distillation of the data down to a number of essential elements which can be expressed in terms of a series of key descriptors and propositions. The intention was to develop an analytic procedure which accounted for all of the data and could be replicated.

The following categories emerged from the pupil interview data:

the pupils' overall impressions of the school (including their first impressions);

the pupils' degree of satisfaction with the school;

comparisons between the pupils' present situation and their experience of other institutions and situations;

the pupils' relationships with other people at the school;

freedom, restrictions, and rules in school; and

pupils' perceptions of the personal effects of their placement

These categories represent the preoccupations expressed by the pupils in interviews and are, therefore, claimed to represent areas of special importance to these pupils.

Findings

1. The Perceived Effects Of Residential Schooling

Pupils showed evidence of improvements in their levels of self-esteem and confidence, based on their own descriptions of the ways in which they had changed since being in the schools:

> The school has helped me grow in myself; helped me go to school [and] get on with my classwork. I'm more confident in myself, being able to do things I never thought I could do.

Others displayed mastery of a wide range of skills (interpersonal, social, academic and practical) which they claimed to have developed as a result of attending the schools.

> Before I came to this school I couldn't do maths or anything. I've improved in everything.

Pupils often claimed to have experienced welcome relief from difficult circumstances they experienced in their home situations (school, family, peer group) as a result of being placed away from home. These circumstances are often closely related to the reasons for their placements:

> It's usually horrible [at home] [...] when our dad's there. He spoils all the fun [...] Some kids love being at home I can't stand it [...] I'm always glad to get back to Lakeside. [...] If I had been at home, and hadn't come here, I'd probably be in the same place where our brother is at the moment [ie prison] [Jock, 17]

Several pupils claimed to have developed deeper understandings of themselves and their personal situations as a result of their residential experience and claimed that this led to improved mastery of their own behaviour, and improvements in their manner of relating to other people, particularly family members:

> This school has given me bit more understanding of life.

> It's straightened me out really.

> Now I don't mess around so much in different situations.

> I think I've improved in my behaviour.

Pupils' perceptions of the academic side of their development varied, those with high academic aspirations complained of the restricted nature of the educational experience provided by the residential schools, in comparison with mainstream schools they had experienced, whilst pupils with learning difficulties claimed to have made academic advances in both schools, owing to the quality of staff support:

> [Being here] has calmed me down [...] it's helped me with my school[work].

A small minority of pupils complained of the stigmatising effect of attending a special boarding-school.

2. Patterns of Organisational Features

Staff in both schools professed to pursue the same list of aims (in order of priority; the last two listed were tied):

to aid pupils' social and emotional development;

to reintegrate pupils into their home situations;

to aid pupils' academic development;

the reintegration of pupils into their local schools;

the preparation of pupils for the world of work.

Staff at Farfield experienced the management style as strong and auto-cratic, and found this to be a source of dissatisfaction, whilst the staff at Lakeside experienced the management style as weak and lacking in direction, and also found this to be a source of dissatisfaction.

The pupils in both schools, however, experienced the management style of staff to be liberal and pupil-centred. Whilst pupils in both schools saw this as desirable, a small subgroup at Lakeside expressed some dissatisfaction, and claimed a preference for the more coercive regime which the recently retired former headmaster had run. Pupil participation in the organisation and running of the schools was common to both institutions, though it took on a more formalised guise at Lakeside. Indeed, there were clear areas of pupil autonomy in both schools (more so however at Lakeside). Similarly, success and achievement in a wide range of areas was acknowledged through the formal privilege and status system in both schools.

In both schools, pupils stated dissatisfaction with aspects of school life which they experienced as depersonalised and dehumanising. They stated, however, that channels existed for their concerns to be aired to the community at large, and valued this.

3. Staff-Pupil Relationships

Staff-pupil relationships in both schools were perceived by both staff and pupils to be characterised by mutual trust and caring. Pupils tended to nominate particular members of staff with whom they had particularly close relationships, or in whom they placed particular trust.

> Before I came here I never used to talk to anyone about my troubles [...] I used to say nothing to no-one when I had a problem. I talk to anyone now. (Jock, 17)

> The staff [here] are more prepared to sit down and talk to you, and talk your problems out. They'll help you out with anything. (Stan, 15)

> Staff will give you more time, if you want to talk to them. Charlie will stay with you, even if he is off duty, until it is sorted out. They have more time for you. (Frank, 16)

Relationships within the pupil-group tended to reflect the positive values identified in staff-pupil relationships, to the extent that pupils engage in informal peer counselling. Staff-pupil relationships formed a central part of the therapeutic purpose of the schools as identified by staff, and the therapeutic effect of the schools as identified by pupils:

> It's [the school] helped me a lot. People I can talk to [...] They've helped me [I've talked about] problems at home. (Alex, 14)

> I treat Mr Brown more as a mate [...]. When he sussed out that I'd got these [stolen] clothes he got slightly worried about it. 'Cos he knows my old dear can't afford all this stuff. So he come to me, and I give him two stories, right. The first time it didn't work. The second time [I said], 'this is the honest truth, sir. you got to believe me now.' The third time, I let it out, 'cos he made me feel so bad when he said, 'right, Ryan, I believe you, but if I find out it's a lie, just don't bother talking to me again.' [...] It was then I thought, shit! I suppose I've got to tell him now, and get it all cleared up. And if I get nicked, I get nicked.' So I told him. (Ryan, 15)

> There was an incident a couple of week ago, where I was piling my plate with food, 'cos I was starving [...] Charlie [a teacher] said, 'leave enough for everyone else!' and with that I just slammed my knife and fork down and walked out! He came after me, after about fifteen minutes, when I'd had a good cry in the bathroom, and said, 'try not to worry too much about what's happening [...]' (Larry, 15)

By and large, pupils valued most highly those staff whom they felt were prepared to listen to them and be sympathetic, and they were less inclined to resist these staff when they made demands on them. Staff whom they perceived to be uncaring were inclined to be the focus for resistance.

4. Forms of Pupil Adaptation

By and large, the pupils showed commitment to the formal values of their schools, judging their own success and progress in terms similar to those used by staff. They appeared to place a high value on improvements in their behaviour and attitudes towards others.

Pupils varied in the extent of their commitment, some being more calculative than others. The most calculative pupils claimed to be motivated to co-operate with the school in order to secure privileges and rewards. Others expressed a commitment to the community, and cited this as a key factor in motivating them to be co-operative with fellow pupils and staff.

Those whose mode of adaptation could be characterised as resistant (a small group at Lakeside) tended to express frustration at the lack of institutional control they experienced. The overwhelming majority of pupils in both schools (including the resistant group) however, claimed to prefer their current placement to other placements that they had experienced.

5. The Resolution of Pupils' Perceived Emotional and Behavioural Difficulties

Evidence from pupils, staff and parents (data obtained in an earlier study carried out at Farfield) indicate progress towards the alleviation of presenting problems which was attributed to the residential experience in particular. Pupils claimed improved mastery and control over their own emotions and behaviour. They also claimed to have developed social and interpersonal skills that enabled them to deal constructively with problem situations (e.g. with parents, peers, teachers) that in the past their reactions would have escalated. They employed these skills to therapeutic effect in their peer relationships in school. An example of improved skills in conflict management was provided by Alex (14):

> I used to argue with my mum. That's all stopped now. There's things that I wouldn't do. Like say I have little argument with my mum now, I'll say sorry to her after. That's one thing I wouldn't even thought of doing when I was at home.

Discussion: Some Theoretical Considerations

Whilst there was evidence of institutionalisation in the two schools, this was not experienced as a major problem by the pupils. Pupils in both schools were subjected to certain 'deprivations' that are associated with institutionalisation, such as curtailments on their freedom of movement and their access to certain privileges which elsewhere might be considered rights. However, these pupils did not suffer the stripping away of their personal identities and consequent dehumanisation that Goffman (1961) describes. On the contrary, it appears that many of these pupils discovered, as a result of the residential experience, new personal identities, which were, for the first time for many of them, a source of pride and satisfaction. The evidence from some of these pupils is that their mainstream school experience had far more of a dehumanising effect than the residential school.

There are three aspects of the residential experience, as described by the pupils of Lakeside and Farfield, that are repeatedly and consistently related to positive outcomes; these are summarised under the headings of *respite, relationships* and *re-signification*. It is argued that these three features of the residential experience are the most critical in achieving the positive outcomes suggested.

A. Respite

A major theme in the pupil interviews was the way in which the residential setting gave them respite from the distressing situations which many encountered in their home settings, in the form of negative family relationships, delinquent peer-group associations and disturbed schooling. These problems can be summarised in terms of economic and social disadvantage, severe emotional tension and discord in the family, and the presence of delinquent influences in the family.

The following quotations give a flavour of the value which pupils in these schools placed on simply being free from family stresses:

> I've settled down with my mum a bit. And I think I've improved a bit [...] as a result of me being away from home. [Jim, 14]

> I think it's got better [his relationship with his mother] because we've spent longer apart. [Ryan, 15]

Respite was also obtained from stresses at their former, mainstream schools and the pupils made reference to unsatisfactory relationships with school staff, the belief that they were victims of inconsistent and unfair treatment by school staff, the belief that they received insufficient personal and academic support from staff, and a perceived inability to tolerate the institutional demands of schools.

Many boys provided accounts of their prior school experience which emphasised intolerance and a sense of being victimised:

> I got kicked out [of a comprehensive school] because I didn't fit in to normal schools [...]. I was messing around in my old school. Like in lessons, I'd start playing around and that in lessons. They was trying to make out that I was worse than I was. Half the time, I was just shouting things out; talking; standing up, things like that. Just walking around like. They'd tell you to get out. Sometimes they'd tell you to get out for a little reason, and I'd say, 'I ain't getting out!' And there starts a fight, with me and a member of staff [...]. Them just dragging me out. They was trying to make out I was worse than I am. (Tom, 15)

> The staff at Lakeside are a lot better. They're more like people! When I was at [day special school], they were more like robots really. You do something wrong, the first thing they do is grab 'em, and stick 'em in a room, and just lock them up! (Arthur, 15)

Some pupils indicated that the schools provided respite from neighbourhood influences, such as peer pressure to engage in delinquent activity:

> Farfield's changed me a lot. If I was at home now, I'd probably be inside or something [...]. I know there's a bunch of kids, some old

mates, who, if I hang around with [them], I'll get nicked [...] But I don't bother hanging around with them no more, because I know it will bodge up my life... Before, I wouldn't have thought of it. (Ryan, 15)

[...] I haven't got any good mates [at home]. They all gets in trouble. (Ian, 14)

It is interesting to note that this range of problems is reflected in the research literature on deviant and disturbed young people (e.g. see West and Farrington, 1973; Dunlop, 1974; Pringle, 1975; Hoghughi, 1978; Tattum, 1982; Rutter and Giller, 1983). Whilst few pupils experience all of these problems, all of the interviewees in this study experienced a combination of some of them.

Particularly prominent were school and family problems. Whilst it would be over-simplistic to think of these problems as 'causes' of EBD, it seems to be the case that for these pupils the experience of having to cope with these circumstances occupied their energies to the exclusion of all else. And often, although the boys themselves were seen by others as being a source of some of these problems, the boys felt powerless to change their behaviour, whilst feeling responsible for it.

The respite provided by the residential situation enabled many of these boys simply to break the cycle of their involvement in these distressing circumstances. Respite in itself was for these pupils a necessary starting point for their positive development, since it gave them relief from circumstances which maintained their problems.

B. Relationships

Relationships of a high quality with staff and fellow pupils in the residential community contributed to the development of more positive self-images by giving pupils a sense of being valued and cared for by significant others whom they learned to trust. Relationships were perhaps the single most important mechanism at work, since it was through relationships that pupils were often first exposed to an image of themselves which challenged their own low opinions of themselves as bad and worthless individuals. It was the reflection of themselves that they saw in others' responses to them that enabled pupils to develop a positive self-image. This in turn gave them the confidence to take on new challenges (educational, social, emotional, etc.) in the knowledge that they would be accepted and valued by others, even if they failed. The following quotation indicates the significance to this pupil of the relationship he shared with his teacher and its perceived effects on his progress:

> I think he [my teacher] helped me quite a bit. He's helped me with my work; talked to me quite a bit. Like I never used to like to go anywhere to do anything. Now I feel quite happy to go to snooker clubs. John [the teacher] takes quite a few of us there. We save our pocket money from the weekend and go there. (Stan, 15)

C. Re-Signification or Positive Signification.

The term 'signification' has been employed by Hargreaves et al (1975) to describe a key component of the process by which pupils come to be labelled as 'deviant'. The term was used by Matza (1976) to describe the point at which an individual's persona becomes identified with a particular form of deviance. It is the process by which a pupil becomes objectified as a 'truant', 'yob', or 'bully'. Signification is when the pupil's deviant acts are taken to be his or her most representative acts. Positive signification occurs when the pupil is labelled with a positive identity. In both cases, the labelling is likely to have the effect of a self-fulfilling prophecy, whereby the pupil comes to internalise the image of him or herself that is projected by others.

Re-signification describes the process that many of the boys in the present study appear to be undergoing in their residential schools. Re-signification involves the development of new and positive identities as a consequence of relationships and experiences which undermine the pupil's original negative view of self, by revealing evidence of desirable, positive qualities. Re-signification is achieved through the availability in these two schools of opportunities for pupils to take on new challenges, learn new skills, develop a deeper knowledge of themselves and move toward a more willing acceptance of themselves.

To succeed, this process depends upon the supportive structure of good quality staff-pupil relationships, a secure environment, as well as the provision of carefully controlled but challenging situations in which effort and success are rewarded and community involvement is encouraged and acknowledged. In its early stages, positive signification involves the rewarding and highlighting of positive attributes that the pupils already possess. For its success, however, it has to be progressive, providing an impetus to take on new challenges.

Conclusions

This chapter has reported a study of two residential schools for pupils with emotional and behavioural difficulties. The study was the first of its kind to focus on pupils' perceptions of the experience and effects of attending such schools. It shows that for the pupils in these two schools the residential experience had many positive outcomes, chief among them being improvements in the pupils' self-images. These improvements are attributed to three major features of the residential experience: respite from problems located in the home situation, the high quality of staff-pupil and pupil-pupil relationships in the schools, and the process of re-signification, which is achieved through a wide range of opportunities for success and achievement in the two schools. It is not claimed that these conclusions refer to anything other than the two schools that were the subject of the study. However, this research offers a basis from which informed hypotheses might be formed, as well as an indication of the shape that future studies of this important, but neglected area might take.

Furthermore, the study offers insights which are of value to mainstream schools. A follow up to the study reported here, looked at a mainstream comprehensive school that was made conspicuous by the dramatic improvements that the school had made in the quality of pupil behaviour, attendance and attainment (see Cooper, 1993a for a full account of this study). It is suggested that the improvements in this school could be accounted for in terms of respite, relationships and positive signification.

These are some of the measures that the mainstream school adopted to achieve these effects:

Respite

In recognition of the fact that many pupils in the school came from chaotic and disorganised home backgrounds, the school placed a high priority on the pastoral work of the school. Central to this endeavour was breaking down what was seen as a 'pastoral-academic divide'. This involved devolving some pastoral responsibilities to all staff and subject departments, whilst giving the pastoral staff responsibilities for monitoring individual pupils' academic progress across the curriculum. This enabled them to pick up early signs of pupil difficulties that might be expressed through a falling off in academic progress. The school also employed a part-time counsellor, who was available on a confidential basis to staff and pupils for individual consultations. An outcome of this arrangement was the development of a peer counselling programme for pupils. In addition to these measures, the old punitive discipline system was replaced by a whole-school discipline code, which set out clear procedures for dealing with discipline problems that emphasised minimal intervention as well as opportunities for pupils and staff to have their perceptions of problem situations aired and explored in a supportive atmosphere.

Relationships

The quality of relationships in the school was seen by the head as a major focus for development as a means toward the end of school improvement. The first issue here was to recognise the relationship between poor staff-pupil relations and low staff morale. The head sought to model the kinds of positive, respectful and supportive relationship she saw as necessary for positive pupil involvement through her own relationships with both staff and pupils. An important feature of this was the restructuring of the senior management team, to include a wider section of the staff. A formal process of consultation on policy matters was also introduced, which revolved around the institution of a programme of workshops involving all staff in which policy issues were debated in small group settings using a problem-solving approach. A key issue here was that staff were not rushed into taking on new developments. When problems had been identified and solutions posited, staff were encouraged to indicate the types of support that they believed they needed in order to implement solutions. It was a common practice for major developments (such as the integration of pupils with SEN) to be 'piloted' on a small scale first of all, usually with volunteer staff. Pupils were also involved in the consultation process through the institution of a school council. Great importance was attached to the development of set of whole school aims that placed the quality of relationships in a position of high priority. This was accompanied by a monitoring and evaluation process to ensure that practice matched rhetoric. Where appropriate, skills training was introduced to assist this process.

Positive Signification

As a counterbalance to the discipline policy a whole-school rewards policy was developed. This was designed to ensure that high level public recognition was available to the whole school population. This involved offering pupils staged rewards for a wide range of activities and qualities both within and outwith the formal curriculum. In addition to this segregationist practices, whereby pupils with special needs and behavioural problems were excluded from the mainstream curriculum, were gradually phased out, and replaced by a system of in-class support. Though again, staff were not rushed into these developments, but were allowed to explore them with support.

It is impossible to do justice to a process that took over five years to complete in a few paragraphs. What is intended here is to show that there are ways of applying some of the underlying principles discussed in this chapter in mainstream schools.

References

Balbernie, R. (1966) *Residential Work with Children* London: Pergamon

Bettelheim, B. (1950) *Love Is Not Enough*. Glencoe, Illinois: The Free Press

Bettelheim, B. (1955) *Truants From Life*. Glencoe, Illinois: The Free Press

Bridgeland, M. (1972) *Pioneer Work with Maladjusted Children*. London: Staples

Burn, M. (1956) *Mr Lyward's Answer*. London: Hamish Hamilton

Cole, T. (1986) *Residential Special Education*. Milton Keynes, Open University

Cooper, P. (1989) *Respite, relationships and re-signification: A study of the effects of residential schooling on pupils with emotional and behavioural difficulties, with particular reference to the pupils' perspective*. Unpublished doctoral dissertation University of Birmingham, Birmingham, England

Cooper, P. (1992) 'Pupils' perceptions of the effects of residential schooling on children with emotional and behavioural difficulties', *Therapeutic Care and Education*, 10, 1

Cooper, P. (1993a) *Effective Schools for Disaffected Students: Integration and Segregation*. London. Routledge

Cooper, P. (1993b) 'Exploring pupils' perceptions of the effects of residential schooling on students with emotional and behavioural difficulties in England', *Child and Youth Care Forum* (USA), 22, 2

Cooper, P. (1993c) 'Learning from the pupil perspective,' *The British Journal of Special Education* 20, 4

Cronk, K. (1987) *Teacher-Pupil Conflict in Secondary Schools*. London: Falmer

Davis, A. (1981) *The Residential Solution*. London: Tavistock

Dawson, R. (1991) The place of four pioneer tenets in modern practice and opinion. *New Growth*, 1 (2), 44- 47

Dawson, R. (1984) Disturbed pupils' perceptions of their teachers' support and strictness. *Maladjustment and Therapeutic Education* , 2(1), 24-27

Dunlop, A. (1970) *The Approved School Experience*. London: HMSO

Glaser, B., and Strauss, A. (1968) *The Discovery of Grounded Theory*. London: Weidenfeld and Nicolson

Grimshaw, P. and Berridge, D. (1994) *Educating Children with Emotional and Behavioural Difficulties*, London: National Children's Bureau

Goffman, E. (1961) *Asylums*. Harmondsworth: Penguin

Hammersley, M., and Atkinson, P. (1983) *Ethnography Principles in Practice*. London: Routledge

Hargreaves, D., Hester, F. and Mellor, F. (1975) *Deviance in Classrooms*. London: Routledge

Hoghughi, M. (1978) *Troubled and Troublesome: Coping with Severely Disordered Children*. London: Burnett Books

Matza, D. (1976) Signification. in P. Hammersley and P. Woods (eds.), *The Process of Schooling*. Milton Keynes, Open University Press

Millham, S., Bullock, R., and Cherrett, P. (1975) *After Grace — Teeth: A comparative study of the residential experience of boys in approved schools*. London: Chaucer

Millham, S., Bullock R., and Hosie, K. (1978) *Locking Up Children: Secure Provision within the Child Care System*, Farnbouough, Saxon House

Mortimore, P., Sammons, L., Stoll, L., and Ecob, R. (1988) *School Matters*. London: Open Books

Neill, A.S. (1916) *A Dominie's Log*. London: Herbert Jenkins

Neill, A S. (1968) *Summerhill*. Harmondsworth, Penguin

Potter, P. (1986) *Long Term Residential Child Care: the Positive Approach*. Norwich: University of East Anglia

Powney, J., and Watts, M. (1987) *Interviewing in Educational Research*. London: Routledge

Pringle, M. (1975) *The Needs of Children*. London: Hutchinson

Purkey, S., and Smith, M. (1983) Effective schools: A review. *The Elementary School Journal*, 83(4), 428-452

Reynolds, D. (1976) The delinquent school. In M. Hammersley and P. Woods (eds.), *The Process of Schooling*. Milton Keynes, Open University

Reynolds, D. (1984) The school for vandals: a sociological portrait of the disaffection prone school. In N. Frude and H. Gault (eds.), *Disruptive behaviour in schools*. Chichester, England: Wiley

Reynolds, D., and Sullivan, M. (1979) Bringing schools back in. In L. Barton and R. Meighan (Eds.), *Schools, Pupils and Deviance*. Nafferton, Nafferton Books

Rogers, C. (1951) *Client Centred Therapy*. London: Constable

Rogers, C. (1980) *A Way of Being*. Boston, MA: Houghton Mifflin

Rosser, E., and Harré, R. (1976) The meaning of trouble. In P. Hammersley and P. Woods (Eds.), *The Process of Schooling*. Milton Keynes, Open University Press

Rutter, M., and Giller, H. (1983) *Juvenile Delinquency: Trends and Perspectives*. Harmondsworth: Penguin

Rutter, M., Maughan, B., Mortimore, P., and Ouston, J. (1979) *Fifteen Thousand Hours*. London: Open Books

Schostak, J. (1983) *Maladjusted Schooling*. London: Falmer

Shaw, O. (1965) *Maladjusted Boys*. London: Allen and Unwin

Shaw, O. (1969) *Prisoners of the Mind*. London: Allen and Unwin

Tattum, D. (1982) *Disruptive Pupils in Schools and Units*. Chichester: Wiley

Wagner Report for the National Institute for Social Work. (1988) *Residential Care: A Positive Choice. Report of the Independent Review of Residential Care*. London: HMSO.

West, D., and Farrington, D. (1973). *Who Becomes Delinquent?* London: Heinemann

Willis, P. (1978) *Learning to Labour*. Aldershot: Gower

Wills,W.D. (1960) *Throw Away Thy Rod*. London: Gollancz

Wittrock, M. (1986) 'Students' thought processes,' in M. Wittrock (ed.), *Handbook of Research on Teaching*. NewYork: Macmillan

Woods, P. (1990) *The Happiest Days? How Pupils Cope with Schools*. London: Falmer

Chapter 7

Former Pupils' Reflections on Residential Special Provision

Tanya Howe

This chapter examines the educational experience of pupils who have been excluded from mainstream provision and placed in residential school as a result of a statement of special educational needs due to emotional and behavioural difficulties. The chapter acknowledges the importance of listening to the views of children and young people concerning their educational experiences and by so doing, gives voice to those who have spent a significant time in a co-educational, residential special school ('Cedarview') in the south of England.

To date, there is a dearth of evidence concerning the efficacy of residential EBD education and even less that draws directly on the views and impressions of those who were educated in such a setting. It is hoped therefore, that this will assist in redressing this shortage and will help inform professionals engaged in such work.

The Study

Thirty-three former pupils (13 males and 20 females) were invited to participate in the study through the completion of a postal questionnaire. Sixty-five per cent of those approached returned completed surveys, in addition, six of the ex-pupils (3 male and 3 female) agreed to be interviewed in some depth about their experiences. These interviews were tape-recorded and transcribed. Subsequent analysis of the interview transcriptions and questionnaire data resulted in the identification of a number of themes which indicated that many of the study participants expressed a range of shared experiences and similar views of the residential special school they attended. The main outcomes and implications of the study are examined under the following headings:

- Respite from negative home-based influences
- Significant interpersonal relationships
- Opportunities for personal achievement
- Preparation for leaving
- Consultation with pupils
- Stigma and institutionalisation
- Resolution of emotional and behavioural difficulties

In the following discussion, fictitious names replace the actual names of the interviewees; verbatim quotations not followed by a name are taken from responses to open-ended questions in the anonymous questionnaire.

Respite from Negative Home-Based Influences

Several of the pupils indicated that they viewed respite from negative influences in their home areas as one of the main benefits of their placement at Cedarview. In response to an open question 11% of the sample identified respite as a central benefit, and four of the six interviewees discussed this feature at some length. The breakdown of relationships with family members, especially parents, emerged as a common source of difficulties as the following comments demonstrate:

I was glad to get away from home. — (Wendy)

It wasn't anywhere near my mother. That was the main benefit — (Jill)

Problems at previous schools and with home-based peers were also noted. Residential placement was regarded as an opportunity to start afresh away from perceived sources of tension. This view was expressed by one of the former pupils interviewed:

> One of the best things about it (Cedarview) was that it gave me the chance to create a new personality for myself. At home in Bourton I was known as a wally or a wimp but going away to boarding school where no-one knew me gave me a fresh start. I was respected at Cedarview whilst I was an outcast in Bourton. (Henry)

This finding supports the results Cooper (1992) obtained from his study of two residential schools. He suggests that residential placement helped many of the boys in his sample:

> ...to simply break the cycle of their involvement in these distressing circumstances. Respite in itself is for these pupils a necessary starting point for their positive development, since it gives them relief from the circumstances which maintain their problems. (page 31)

Some participants of the current study suggested that they missed out on important aspects of family life as a result of attending Cedarview and that they returned to difficult family situations during holiday periods and on leaving school. There was however, some indication that, as a result of developing maturity and increased self-reliance, participants were able to cope with these difficulties more effectively. It was also apparent that many of the former pupils felt that the quality of liaison between school staff and parents was far from satisfactory. Over half of those surveyed (57%) considered there was insufficient contact between their parents and school staff. A few participants clearly regretted the effect long periods away from home had on family relationships:

> I know my parents felt very left out.

> Losing contact on a day-to-day basis with your parents means you miss out on stages of a parent-child relationship.

> ...I spent the most important part of my youth away from my home life.

A small number of participants suggested that their family-based difficulties were not solved in the long term:

> If your problem is in the family it all starts again when you leave.

> I grew up not feeling loved and it has carried through to my adult life.

Reflecting on his placement, Henry indicated that removing him from his family, whilst providing much-needed respite, failed to resolve the difficulties between himself and his mother in the long term:

> The problems between me and my mother stayed the same. She still doesn't admit it now. She tells people I went to the school because I had problems with my school work. Things are now better but that is only because I grew up. At the time both sides needed help: me and my family. All they did was to split us up but I still went back there in the holidays and that was quite difficult.

These findings suggest that whilst it provides an excellent starting point, respite must operate alongside other forms of treatment if long-term improvements in pupils' interpersonal relationships and circumstances are to be effected beyond the immediate environment of the residential school. The needs of the family must be viewed in tandem with those of the pupil attending residential school and, despite the difficulties associated with maintaining contact over large geographical distances, the development of good working relationships with pupils' families must be a central objective of the effective residential EBD school.

Significant Interpersonal Relationships

The development of good quality interpersonal relationships emerged as one of the main benefits of time spent at Cedarview. Since pupils placed in this form of educational provision have almost invariably experienced long-term problems in sustaining appropriate interpersonal relationships prior to referral, this finding is particularly important. Similar evidence was gathered in earlier studies conducted by Wilson and Evans (1980) and Cooper (1992) who suggest that the development of high quality interpersonal relationships is central to the enhancement of pupils' self-esteem which is generally very low at the time of referral to an EBD boarding school.

In the current study few references were made to friendships with specific peers. Rather the emphasis was on the way in which the organisation of the school along the lines of a large family unit afforded plentiful opportunities for pupils to work co-operatively. This is evident in the following accounts of everyday life at Cedarview described by two interviewees:

> We used to get the same team on washing-up. We used to organise it so that one person done pans that liked doing them, one liked to wash-up and one to dry... You could get an evening's washing-up done in 20 minutes. — (Charles)

> I remember when we went to the Bath and West Show and got absolutely drowned and the school cellar drowned. We had like a chain getting all the water out. It was absolutely brilliant and we just really pulled together. — (Pamela)

Other school-based activities, including sports days, dramatic productions and caring for animals were recalled as situations which promoted social interaction between staff and pupils. It was clear that many of the former pupils believed that the ethos of the school contributed towards the development of warm, caring interpersonal relationships. The small size of the school and the relaxed atmosphere were viewed positively by the pupils.

Few references were made to individual relationships with school-based peers. The fact that 71% of those surveyed however, currently maintain contact with at least one of their contemporaries indicates that lasting relationships were established. Thirty-one percent of those questioned identified losing contact with home-based peers as a disadvantage of residential placement:

> It was hard to go home. I lost touch with people in my home area.

> Feeling isolated when at home in the holidays.

This was evidently a long term problem since over half (52%) of the sample admitted to experiencing problems in establishing friendships in their home area on leaving school.

Whilst it was stated that physical bullying took place only occasionally, there were detailed descriptions of the existence of a hierarchical structure which pupils and staff recognised. This is demonstrated in the following interview extracts:

> There wasn't bullying in my time at Cedarview because there was a tremendous amount of respect for the staff and the older pupils. If you were out of line then they (older pupils) dealt with you, not by bullying, by saying that this is not right. It was like everyone else used to not speak to you or they would cause a scene so that you would not do it again. — (Pamela)

> There were lots of cliquey groups and you knew your place. There were hierarchies. The pecking order was very marked and kids controlled each other... The staff actually acknowledged the pecking order and reinforced it. I think that was because it made life easier for them. — (Henry)

Three of the former pupils interviewed talked in some detail about the co-educational status of the school. All considered it a positive feature since it provided opportunities for pupils to develop appropriate relationships with peers of both sexes. Co-education can however, generate problems and the following accounts provide an insight into some of the personal difficulties encountered:

> It was generally good that it was mixed. It taught you to interact with members of the opposite sex. It was more natural. I was introduced to sex very young, starting at the age of about 13. It was a very difficult thing to control and I didn't realise all the implications... Looking back on it now I suppose there was a lot of it going on because a lot of us were looking for the love we had not got from our parents. — (Henry)

> It would have been rather bitchy and catty if it had been an all girls school... As I say I had a problem with males so being mixed helped really. I couldn't hide away from it so it helped me face up to it. — (Pamela)

Good quality, informal relationships with members of staff were highly valued and the questionnaire data showed that as many as 90% of the respondents were in contact with current and former members of staff at the time of the study. This is particularly significant, since the school has no official support network to offer pupils once they leave the school.

A number of comparisons were made between the quality of staff- pupil relationships enjoyed at Cedarview and those experienced in mainstream schools. Participants felt that the warm, informal relationships fostered at Cedarview were more helpful than the impersonal, authoritarian ones typical of ordinary schools they had attended. This is demonstrated in the following extract where Jill compares her experiences of teachers:

> It's a lot less formal... I mean like teachers in mainstream schools say, 'If you've got problems you can come and talk to me'. What bullshit! I suppose it's a lot easier in this type of school isn't it? Because there is not such a big distance between us... And it's first names as well, which helps. That in itself makes it less formal. And they are more like human beings. Teachers in normal schools are so straight and upright and all sort of high and mighty, aren't they?

Other responses identified the development of trust, learning to accept responsibility and being valued as individuals as important aspects of staff-pupil relationships. The importance of staff as role models was highlighted. Forty-one per cent of the respondents answered an open question designed to explore negative aspects of residential placement related to perceived unfair treatment from members of staff. Fourteen per cent of the replies to this question referred specifically to a lack of consultation between staff and pupils, including not being informed of important decisions and personal concerns being treated lightly:

> When some of our friends were being sent home (suspended) and the staff tried to keep us occupied while they left because we didn't know and they thought we would make a big fuss.

> Feeling that I wasn't being taken seriously about not wanting to stay at my mother's...and subsequent holiday arrangements, or lack of them.

Evidence that the behaviour of staff was viewed critically by pupils is supported by the following interview extracts concerning inconsistent treatment of pupils and the bad example set by staff who smoked openly in front of children:

> There was an amazing amount of blatant favouritism. — (Henry)

Another thing I don't think they should have done was encouraging people to smoke... Some of the staff used to smoke in front of the children. Now that is classed as passive smoking... I mean I don't think teachers or care staff should smoke when there's kids around. — (Charles)

It is clear that maintenance of good staff-pupil relations rests on the dedication, consistency and ability of staff to command respect through setting good examples to the pupils in their care. In support of this, Laslett (1977) states that the presence of predictable and reliable members of staff who are able to provide pupils with much needed stability and security is an essential feature of an effective residential EBD school. There are obvious implications here concerning staff selection procedures and the provision of appropriate in-service training and support networks for staff engaged in this demanding work.

Opportunities for Personal Achievement

In response to an open question exploring the benefits of residential placement, 31% of the comments related to opportunities for the enhancement of self-esteem whilst a further 26% focused specifically on educational progress and academic achievements. In addition, 21% of the answers to a separate question investigating 'good memories' of time spent at Cedarview were characterised by accounts of personal achievements. Comparing residential with mainstream schooling, the small teaching groups and provision of individual help from teachers were viewed as positive features of the education available at Cedarview:

You got much more attention. There were less in a class. I passed quite a few exams really didn't I?... I was quite surprised. — (Wendy)

Cedarview helped me to handle situations more clearly. I learned more because the teachers did not have overcrowded classes and had more time to give individuals.

All of those surveyed enjoyed success in some public examinations. Several felt that whilst there would have been a wider range of curricular opportunities at ordinary schools it was unlikely that they would have aspired to the same academic levels as those they reached at Cedarview. Table 1 indicates the numbers of exam passes gained and includes GCSE grades A to G, CSE grades 1 to 5 and '0' Level grades A to E

Table 1 Examination passes

(20 respondents)

No. of passes	%
Nil	5
1	25
2 or 3	10
4 or 5	45
More than 5	15

It is interesting to note that 60% of this sample achieved the equivalent of four or more GCSE. passes. National figures show that 82.2% of all 16 year-olds gained at least five GCSEs at grades A to G in 1991/2. Unfortunately separate examination results indicating the performance of pupils in EBD provision are unavailable.

The wide range of extra-curricular activities available at the school was viewed by some participants as one of the main benefits of placement. Some indicated that they enjoyed a range of enriching experiences that would have been unavailable to them if they had not attended the school. Data gathered in response to a question asking participants to give details of extra- curricular activities they enjoyed at Cedarview is shown in Table 2.

Table 2 Extra-Curricular Activities

Activities	%
Sports	64
Animal Care	16
Outings	11
Drama and Dance	9

Several interviewees talked of opportunities they found rewarding:

> When you are at boarding schools you go out on outings, right, which you would not have chance or even any way of doing otherwise... I wouldn't have gone to discos or anything like that, like I have done at Cedarview... You got to meet a lot more people ... We got to travel and see things that we wouldn't normally be able to afford to go and see, like 'Joseph and the Amazing Technicolour Dreamcoat'.' — (Edward)

That was another thing I got out of it, animals. I used to ride a bit before I went there but at Cedarview it was more sort of looking after them. I enjoyed that a lot. It was something I never would do otherwise because I could never have had my own horse or anything. — (Jill)

Two of the interviewees spoke with enthusiasm about their involvement in caring for the donkeys and horses. The therapeutic benefits of these experiences and the way in which their interest in the animals enabled them to assume increasing responsibility as they grew older are significant features of their accounts:

By the time I was a bit older and I was sort of more responsible and more trusted I could do quite a bit you know. There was quite a bit of responsibility and I did quite a few things... I just used to go and talk to them when I was pissed off. Having the animals there makes it less institutionalised. You know, with a dog stretched out in the middle of the passage. It's something that lots of kids haven't had because of their backgrounds — (Jill)

Being responsible for animals when you are a child is a good thing because you aren't just involved with people. You've got to learn to care for other things as well and also it is easier to love animals than it is to love yourself. I think that by having animals around it was a kind of thing that one could get involved in and communicate with and sort of like calm you down and you can relate to, which really helped with our behaviour problems at the time. I know I always used to feel different when I was with the animals because I felt that I was doing a responsible job and I just loved being around them. — (Pamela)

Sporting activities, the annual 'School Social' and the termly dance and drama productions were remembered fondly for the sense of togetherness they engendered and the opportunities they provided for the enhancement of pupils' self-esteem. This is demonstrated in the following selection of responses to an open question asking participants to recall a 'good memory' of their placement:

Being the captain of most of the sports teams.

Winning the swimming gala.

Being given the leading role in a school production. This helped me to believe in myself and gave me confidence.

I guess it was the first time I appeared as the lead in a ballet. It made me feel special for the first time ever.

These findings indicate that through the provision of a range of enriching experiences residential placement provided these pupils with opportunities to interact socially, enjoy personal successes and begin to develop a sense of self-worth, sometimes for the first time in their lives. Similarly, many of the boys in Cooper's (1993) study developed enhanced self-images as a result of experiencing personal achievement in a range of spheres and through taking an active part in the life of the community. Wilson and Evans (1980) also found that the provision of opportunities for pupils to enjoy individual successes was a central feature of the 'best practice' residential EBD schools they surveyed.

Preparation for Leaving

Evidence emerged from the study suggesting that the curriculum at Cedarview failed to prepare pupils to face the challenges of the outside world on leaving school. Seventeen and a half percent of the participants felt that they were not equipped with the self-help skills necessary for independent survival in the community and perceived this as a major disadvantage of their residential placement. It was suggested that pupils were allowed to remain overdependent on staff right up to the time of leaving and that this resulted in adaptation problems when independence was suddenly thrust upon them. This view is demonstrated clearly in the following response to an open question investigating the disadvantages of residential placement:

It was very difficult to get used to life without contact with the supportive relationships I had for five years. I found making a life away from the school a slow process as all my thoughts were there. The sheltered environment school offers makes leaving and facing the world outside difficult.

The inadequacy of the Careers Guidance available at Cedarview was highlighted as a common source of dissatisfaction. Responses to the question, 'What did you think of the Careers Guidance you were offered at school?' are shown in Table 3.

Table 3 Usefulness of Guidance

(21 responses)

Rating	%
Excellent	9
Quite useful	19
Useless	24
Can't remember being given any guidance	48

Problems associated with the development of effective leavers' schemes in residential EBD schools are documented by Cole (1986). He cites the geographical distance between the school and many pupils' homes as a major factor limiting the scope of these programmes. The results of the current study identify a need for staff at Cedarview to devise a comprehensive programme incorporating life-skills and independence training, work experience and careers guidance with a view to enabling pupils to progress towards independent living during their final two years of schooling.

In contrast to the evidence presented above, several participants described how residential placement fostered personal qualities which had helped them to cope with the demands of life in the community and family pressures since leaving school. The development of self-reliance and coping skills were regarded as central long-term benefits:

> Basically it (Cedarview) did sort my head out and I really learned to stand on my own two feet. — (Wendy)

> The one thing that Cedarview taught me was to stick up for myself. — (Henry)

> There has always been some sort of self-survival in me and I think that is what the school provided in some way. — (Pamela)

Consultation with Pupils

Most of the participants were satisfied with the extent to which pupils were involved in the day-to-day running of the school. Several respondents explained that pupils were encouraged to accept responsibilities in a variety of ways including animal care and domestic tasks and to make their views and ideas known via the daily school meeting:

I liked the idea of the meeting everyday...The fact that you had a say in what was going on in the school. — (Charles)

Questionnaire participants were asked, 'As a pupil, to what extent do you feel you were consulted and involved in decision-making concerning plans for your future?' The mixture of responses collected is shown in Table 4.

Table 4 Extent of Consultation

(21 responses)

Consultation	%
Consulted when near leaving	43
Sometimes consulted	29
Always consulted	14
Never consulted	14

The data gathered here indicate that pupils became more involved in personal decision-making as they approached school-leaving age and compares favourably with the results of a recent study by Keys and Fernandes (1993) of two thousand Year 7 and 9 pupils attending mainstream schools. They found that only 6 to 7% of their sample reported having discussed their progress regularly with teachers during the previous year. Whilst pupil consultation is a relatively new concept to the education service in general, it has long been a central feature of therapeutic communities and some residential schools where pupils are actively involved in the day-to-day running of the units in which they live (Cole 1986).

Stigma and Institutionalisation

Since stigma associated with residential placement is frequently reported (Galloway and Goodwin 1979, Topping 1983) as a disadvantage of residential education, it seemed appropriate to explore participants' perceptions of this issue. Table 5 shows the response to the question, 'If a friend you had recently met asked you about your education, how would you react?'

Table 5 How education referred to

(21 responses)

Reaction	%
Just say I went to boarding school	48
Explain about type of school and reasons for my placement	38
Explain about type of school and leave it at that	14

These results show that a large proportion of the participants are currently, as adults, reluctant to discuss their schooling openly. The following interview extract indicates that residential placement can result in long-term, negative labelling. Pamela explained that during an interview for a college place her former education at a residential EBD school generated some discussion regarding her suitability as a candidate for a place on a Child Care course:

So when I was 23 and applied for college I was horrified because you get labelled...There is a stigma and there are certain friends you (researcher) know that feel the same way... It's like, I suppose being an ex-convict or something like that.' -(Pamela)

Several participants identified a stigma associated with segregated educational provision which continues to affect them in adulthood. The data collected indicate that many of the former pupils questioned have suffered the effects of negative labelling as a result of their placements and remain guarded when discussing attendance at a residential school with current acquaintances. Similarly, many of the ex-pupils questioned in Laslett's study (1985) perceived the stigma associated with placement as an enduring negative feature of residential education.

Difficulties associated with living in an institution were identified as negative features of residential placement. In response to an open question exploring the disadvantages of attending a residential school, 27.5% of the comments related to institutional living. In particular, *a lack of privacy, petty rules, rigid and impersonal routines and insufficient opportunities to engage in activities in the local community* were identified as common disadvantages. Specific examples mentioned included *collecting clothes at certain times, communal washing facilities and sparsely furnished dormitories.* The following responses relate to this aspect of the residential experience:

> You don't see the real world as much as you should.

> Lack of communication with the outside world in all aspects.

> There was no place you could go to be alone... It has made me very institutionalised in many ways... I find it difficult to make decisions.

> If I had an argument with someone I couldn't get away from them.

Table 6 indicates that shopping trips to the nearby town, attending the local Youth Club and disco, and visiting other schools for sports fixtures were the main opportunities for pupils to develop social contacts outside the school premises.

Table 6 Outside Contact

(46 responses)

Contact	%
Shopping	37
Social Events	26
Sports Matches	22
College Link Courses	7
No outside contact	4
Work Experience	2
Pub (unofficially)	2

There seems to be a connection between the negative labelling of pupils and the ignorance of the general public concerning the nature of modern residential EBD schools. Even education professionals who are not directly involved in this sector, know little of the work of these establishments (Cooper 1993). The isolated location of many of these schools together with the residential factor conjures up images of separation and alienation traditionally associated with institutions, in the minds of the general public. The outcome is that links between these schools and local communities are often, at best, tenuous. In an effort to address these difficulties, the staff of residential EBD schools need to promote a wider awareness of their work by opening their doors to the general public. In addition to welcoming them to school-based social events, consideration needs to be given to making school facilities, for example, sports pitches and swimming pools available to local residents at certain times with a view to eroding barriers, creating more realistic perceptions of the work of residential schools and developing mutually supportive relationships between schools and their communities.

In recent years, minimising institutional effects has been a priority at Cedarview. Staff are promoting a policy of integrating pupils into the wider community by providing a range of opportunities for participation in activities outside the school. At present these include work experience placements, college link courses, sports matches with mainstream and special schools, Duke of Edinburgh Award Scheme, youth clubs and discos.

Resolution of Emotional and Behavioural Difficulties

Perhaps the most significant findings of the study were those associated with pupils' levels of awareness concerning two central issues: the type of school they were attending and individual reasons for placement. The survey results indicate that 71% of the respondents were unaware that they were being placed at a residential EBD school at the time of their referral. Even more surprising perhaps is the evidence presented in Table 7, which demonstrates that a significant proportion of the sample remained ignorant of the form of provision they were experiencing throughout their entire placement. In response to a closed question asking those participants who were unaware of the nature of the school at the time of referral when they became aware of its type, the following data were collected:

Table 7 Awareness of Nature of Placement
(15 responses)

When becoming aware	%
Shortly after admission	27
Over a year after admission	20
Since leaving the school	33
As a result of this survey	7
No response	13

One of the interviewees who was sexually abused as a young child referred to her lack of awareness concerning the school type and the feelings she experienced when she later discovered that she had attended a special school:

> Many of the kids had problems and for different reasons. But I didn't know that it was a maladjusted school when I went there. That was difficult to... When I found out what the school was really about I was quite angry then that the school didn't do more to find out really what my problems really were. — (Pamela)

These findings identify inadequacies in the statementing and referral processes and the induction programme in operation at the school. The implications are that pupils are insufficiently prepared for residential placement and that they are deprived of vital information concerning their education. It is interesting to note that Grimshaw and Berridge (1993) similarly found that pupils generally were not actively encouraged to take part in the process of referral to the four residential EBD schools they studied.

Most respondents indicated that they knew very little of the reasons for their placements at the time of referral. Since many of those surveyed were very young and no doubt distressed at the time of initial placement, a lack of understanding or confusion concerning the circumstances surrounding placement may be expected. What is perhaps more difficult to explain however, is the set of results presented in Table 8. These indicate that, as adults, a significant percentage of the sample still do not know why they were placed in this form of provision. Participants were asked to comment on the reasons for their placement at a residential school.

Table 8 Perceptions of Reasons for Placement
(35 responses)

Reasons	%
Don't know the reasons	40
School-based difficulties	37
Family-based problems	20
In trouble with the police	3

The following responses to this question refer to participants' ignorance of factors contributing to their placement:

I always wanted to know and asked the school several times to look at my records, but I was told that I was not allowed.

I have never been entirely sure as to why I was sent to Cedarview.

I was fully unaware of the behaviour I was giving out and why until my early twenties.

It is possible that a partial explanation lies in the school philosophy. It is believed that children who have lived through a series of distressing experiences need space and time to make a fresh start away from unnecessary pressures when they join the school. Whilst counselling is available, the negative effects of past experiences are addressed mainly on the instigation of pupils. It is suggested that problems can be resolved satisfactorily only when pupils feel they are strong enough to face them and that some are most effectively dealt with after leaving school. There is some suggestion that when too much attention is focused on pupils' problems their difficulties may be exacerbated. Since past events cannot be altered, emphasis at Cedarview is placed upon developing a positive attitude to the future. Helping pupils to find effective methods of meeting the challenges of life's experiences is viewed as the central task.

In the light of this discussion it is not surprising that some participants felt that their emotional and behavioural difficulties were not alleviated as a result of attending Cedarview. In answer to an open question investigating former pupils' views on this aspect of the residential experience, 15% of those surveyed felt the school did not help them come to terms with their problems at all and 27% were apparently unaware of the existence of their emotional and behavioural difficulties. Responses falling into the latter category indicate that some participants externalised their problems by citing family members or previous school-based issues as the root causes:

What problems? My parents were my problem, I wasn't.

I was not aware I had a problem.

I did not know I had been sent to Cedarview because I had problems. When it came apparent to me that all the kids were at Cedarview for some reason, I then thought about my reason.

Cole (1986) presents an alternative philosophy from that promoted at Cedarview concerning the resolution of pupils' emotional and behavioural difficulties. He suggests:

> it is essential that a child's unacceptable behaviour be confronted and criticised. Aspects of a child's character which might be painful to him must be examined and the child helped to understand the nature of his disturbance. (page 45)

This approach is supported by the comments made during one of the interviews. The interviewee believed that pupils could only begin to come to terms with their difficulties after they had accepted ownership of their problems. Later in the conversation he outlined the importance of reality confrontation by explaining how his own unrealistic career aspirations were reinforced by school staff with the result that he was unprepared for the level of competition he faced in the world beyond the protection of the school environment:

> You got the idea that the level you were at in the school was the same as it would be when you got out. This is not true. You might be one of the best in the school but outside loads of people are better. Like I wanted to be a policeman at one time and the teachers encouraged me to think that I could. I don't think they should do that. They should help you come to terms with reality. — (Henry)

Conclusions

A number of themes were generated from the analysis of data gathered during this study. In summary, initial respite, rewarding interpersonal relationships and personal achievements resulting in enhanced self-esteem may be identified as the main benefits of residential placement. The negative effects of isolation from families and local communities, insufficient preparation for leaving school and incomplete resolution of emotional and behavioural difficulties emerge as weaknesses of this form of special educational provision. The high level of ignorance shared by many of the study participants regarding the type of school in which they were placed and spent a significant part of their schooling, together with the lack of awareness of the reasons leading to their referral, are probably the most significant findings of this study and indicate an area worthy of more detailed investigation. It is important to stress that the findings represent the views of twenty-one former pupils who attended Cedarview at a particular period of time. It is not intended that the outcomes of the study should be generalised to other residential settings or, indeed, be assumed to represent the perceptions of pupils currently placed at the school.

This research was based on the belief that important insights into the effectiveness of EBD provision could be gained by examining pupils' perspectives, since as clients of the service, they hold the key to unique and highly personal accounts regarding the experience of residential special schooling. A research framework was developed which was constrained by the time the researcher, as a full time teacher in the school, had to conduct the study and by the ethical and professional dilemmas encountered. These included the problems associated with the respective roles of teacher and researcher. The selection of the sample and the choice of postal questionnaires and semi-structured interviews as research tools involved a great deal of deliberation and a degree of risk concerning the quantity and quality of the data obtained. Other considerations centred on the risks associated with conducting research which delved deeply into potentially sensitive and painful issues with a group which included former pupils and current friends of the researcher.

Examples of the rich data collected in the study are presented in this chapter and demonstrate the value of adopting the pupil's perspective and the benefits of employing a combination of quantitative and qualitative research methods and the suitability of this approach for teacher-researchers conducting small-scale studies. Problems associated with the development of appropriate research frameworks have long contributed to the lack of empirical studies undertaken in this field. The current negative profile of residential EBD provision heightens the need for further research investigating the effectiveness of residential special schools. Since economic pressures are likely to continue to prohibit centrally funded research programmes for the foreseeable future, the task of raising the profile and improving the quality of this form of educational provision rests largely with individual practitioners.

Bibliography

Cole, T. (1986) *Residential Special Education*. Milton Keynes, Open University Press.

Cooper, P. (1992) 'Exploring Pupils' Perceptions of the Effects of Residential Schooling on Children with Emotional and Behavioural Difficulties'. *Therapeutic Care and Education*, 1 (1), 22-34.

Cooper, P. (1993) *Effective Schools for Disaffected Students: Integration and Segregation*. London, Routledge.

Galloway, D. and Goodwin, C. (1979) *Educating Slow-learning and Maladjusted Children*. London, Longman.

Grimshaw, R. and Berridge, D. (1993) *The Placement and Progress of Children in Residential Special Schools for Emotional and Behavioural Difficulties: A Summary of Project Findings*. Paper issued at National Children's Bureau Conference, March 31st 1993.

Keys, W. and Fernandes, C. (1993) *What Do Students Think About School?* Slough, NFER.

Laslett, R. (1977) *Educating Maladjusted Children*. St Albans, Granada Publishing.

Laslett, R. (1985) 'A Follow-up Study of Children Leaving Three Residential Schools for the Maladjusted'. *Maladjustment and Therapeutic Education*, 3 , 13-19.

Topping, K. (1983) *Educational Systems for Disruptive Adolescents*. London, Croom Helm.

Wilson, M. and Evans, M. (1980) *Education of Disturbed Pupils*, London, Methuen.

Chapter 8

Exploring Pupils' Perceptions of their Experience in Secure Accommodation

Philip Colville Craig

This chapter is concerned with an examination of the views of ten young people, who were being detained in a secure unit under Section 53 of the Children and Young Persons' Act (1933), about their educational and care experiences. They had all committed offences which, if they had been adults, could have resulted in sentences of fourteen years or more imprisonment. These include murder, manslaughter, arson and rape. The centre also accommodates some young offenders on remand and absconders from other social welfare establishments. In 1995, there are one hundred and twenty seven young people in England and Wales who are detained under this section of the 1933 Act and there are approximately three hundred places available in secure accommodation for those young people deemed by the law to be either a danger to the public and/or to themselves.

Despite widespread distaste at the incarceration of children, there is an acceptance that there will always be a small number of young people for

133

whom it will be necessary to provide secure containment. As Harris and Timms (1993) state, young delinquents need to be helped as well as punished. The emphasis will be decided on an individual basis as determined by legal and professional opinion. This means that secure accommodation is a 'fundamentally ambiguous facility' (p.4), a view shared by Cawson and Martell (1979) and Ditchfield and Catan (1992). This conflict between the recognition of the need for treatment and the feeling that society requires punishment and retribution for wrong-doing, is an issue which is central to the care and rehabilitation of young offenders in secure accommodation.

Methods of enquiry

This enquiry was conducted through the use of a combination of data-gathering tools. Semi-structured interviews were planned, along with an analysis of each interviewee's personal file. This, coupled with the fact that the author was also actively teaching each of the pupils, ensured that a high degree of interviewer/interviewee familiarity was present. A key principle which should underpin all interpretative studies is that of 're-flexivity' (Hammersley and Atkinson 1983). Reflexivity refers to the researcher's need to be aware of the effect that he is having on the situation under investigation. Reflexivity was of particular relevance to this study as the author was, at that time, teaching in the secure unit under consideration.

Howe (1993) felt 'considerable unease regarding the ethical implications of involving current pupils in research' (p.30). She decided not to interview current pupils at her school and felt that 'The confidentiality and intimate field relationships which are essential to good research practice may create tension and place a strain on existing relationships between the teacher researcher and her colleagues as well as pupils' (p.30).

Cooper (1992) however, did interview pupils at his school and felt that the 'relative informality" (p.6) of the small, residential school setting and its emphasis on fairly informal, co-operative relationships between staff and pupils made the situation less problematic than it might have been. Similar considerations were fundamental to this study also.

Each pupil was provided with a summary of the information obtained. This course of action offered each interviewee the opportunity to clarify any point or to add further information. This additional interview was also used to focus upon issues which had emerged from the data.

No attempt is made to generalise the results of this investigation. The study was exploratory relying heavily upon semi-structured interviewing techniques. The results of this study represent only the views of the pupils interviewed. It is the author's opinion, however, that idiographic studies of this nature can provide valid and detailed descriptions of social settings which can then lead to nomothetic investigations and the ability to generalise.

Although much of the data obtained by this investigation is essentially qualitative in nature, there was also a significant amount of quantitative data produced by way of responses to nominal and ordinal scales of measurement. In the semi-structured interviews, for example, pupils were first asked to respond either 'Yes' or 'No' to questions and were then asked to explain why they answered in that way.

The following themes emerged from the semi-structured personal interview data as the most salient aspects of the pupils' experience:

The pupils' feelings when they were first told that they were going to be sent to secure accommodation (including their first impressions)

The pupils' preconceptions of what a secure unit would be like and the prevalent fear of being bullied

The pupils' views on whether or not they needed to be in secure accommodation

The pupils' perceptions on the concept of punishment

What the pupils hoped to achieve during their stay in secure accommodation.

The pupils' past educational experience and their current views on education.

The pupils' plans for the future when they leave secure accommodation and whether or not they feel they will re-offend.

The pupils' opinions on how the secure experience could be improved.

1. First reactions to placement.

All ten respondents experienced negative feelings when they were first told that they were going to be sent to secure accommodation but five of them also stated that they had experienced ambivalence, in that whilst they did not necessarily want to be placed in a secure unit, they were relieved that they were not going to be sent to, or to remain in, prison. Five of the ten individuals had been remanded in prisons because no places in secure units were available for them. One young man who was in the dock at Crown Court when he first found out he was to be placed in security felt:

> ... light-headed, dizzy, worried. wanted to cry but couldn't — thought I was going to die. Relieved about not going to prison but thought there would be pressure on me from both staff and kids.

Another young man admitted to being drunk in a police station when he first found out. His social worker told him and he felt:

> upset, gutted, confused, frightened — wondered where the hell I was going to. Felt I was being shifted from pillar to post.

A third respondent said that he was:

> relieved, because I was remanded in prison and nothing is worse than prison but I was worried too because I thought I might get bullied in secure.

A fourth interviewee found out in a police station but was then remanded to Cardiff Prison for a week until a place was available for him. He said he felt physically sick. He cried and:

> ...couldn't believe this was happening to me, wanted to run but couldn't. I felt really choked. I was shaking. It didn't seem real, like a nightmare.

Upon analysis of these responses it was evident that, in the maelstrom of emotion surrounding such a decision, there was one powerful emotion missing — anger. Not one respondent stated that they were angry about being deprived of their liberty. When interviewed, they admitted to being 'upset', 'frightened', 'confused', 'anxious', 'choked' and 'gutted' but not angry.

The pupils were also asked about their feelings when they first arrived in secure accommodation and what, if anything, was done by staff to make them feel more at ease with their situation. Six of the ten young men remembered feeling scared. One said that the secure unit:

> ... was scary-looking. It looked like a dungeon: horrible, dark, depressing. Even my social worker said it looked depressing. I was worried — thought I might be bullied.

Another concurred with this view:

> What a dirty place from the outside — grubby, depressing. I just wanted to get banged in my room — bit frightened, scared of bullying — didn't want to meet the other kids because of the nature of my offence.

However, two respondents expressed positive feelings when they first arrived in the secure unit. One stated that he felt:

> ... good, because the staff were friendly and helpful — not like prison at all!

Another felt:

> OK, because I knew one of the kids here and he told me it was safe here and because I didn't have to go back to Gloucester Prison.

The other two interviewees had never lived away from home before. One remembered being very upset and 'homesick' whilst the other felt 'weird about living somewhere new'.

Eight out of the ten respondents felt that staff did their best to ease any worries that they had. One young man stated:

> staff showed me all around the unit, introduced me to the other kids, spent a lot of time with me, let me 'phone home ... were friendly.

Another felt that members of staff:

> ... gave me attention, talked to me, told me not to worry, told me not to talk about my offence, gave me a booklet about the place, encouraged me to join in activities.

The two young men who felt that staff did not do their best to ease their worries did not, in fact, allow them to attempt to make them feel better.

Both individuals were frightened, scared of being bullied and wanted to be locked in their rooms because of the nature of their offences.

The findings also confirmed that many secure accommodation placements occur in emergencies and the planning that is universally deemed fundamental to good child care and social work practice is often impossible (Harris and Timms, 1993).

All of the respondents were either in a police station, court or prison when they were first informed that they were to be placed in secure accommodation. Planning and emergencies do not coexist comfortably and it was obvious that these secure placements were as a result of sudden traumatic occurrences in the pupils' lives and very often, in the lives of others.

In addition, the findings concerning the emotional state of the pupils when first being told that they were to be sent to secure accommodation and their subsequent first impressions of the secure unit, have profound implications for admission procedure. All ten interviewees experienced negative feelings and six admitted to being scared. Eight of the ten pupils felt that staff did their best to ease their worries by being friendly, spending time with them, introducing them to peers and other staff, letting them 'phone home and generally talking to them about the unit and their situations. Two individuals, however, were too upset and confused to allow themselves to be treated in this way. They needed some time alone in order to come to terms with their situation and were not ready to be introduced to the unit and its ways. It is vital therefore, that any admission procedure policy be flexible enough to recognise that being placed in security is a traumatic experience and different individuals react in varying ways and need to be treated accordingly.

2. Perceptions of life in a secure unit

Eight of the ten respondents had never been in a secure unit before and had never lived away from home. Their main fear was that of being bullied, seven pupils stated this explicitly. Typical responses were:

I thought there would be pressure on me from staff and kids.

I thought it would be like 'Scum' the film: bullying, violence, drugs — but it's not. There's hardly any of that at all. I thought it would be much harder than this.

I just wanted to get banged up in my room. I was a bit frightened, scared of bullying didn't want to meet the other kids because of the nature of my offence.

I was scared stiff of being bullied. I've been bullied before and thought it would be really bad in a secure unit.

A second anxiety concerned the type of regime that would operate in secure accommodation. All ten interviewees stated that the secure unit in which they were placed was not as strict as they thought it would be. One young man said:

I thought we'd be locked up in our rooms all day, maybe allowed out for an hour a day. Here we're out of our rooms from 7.30 am until 9.30 pm — but you can go to your bedroom if you want some peace and quiet.

... if you were naughty the staff would stick you in a padded cell for about three hours at a time. My Dad was in a secure unit, and he used to be beaten with a cane.'

A third imagined that the regime would be much harsher:

I thought it would be like Borstal — violent, crap meals, staff would be a lot stricter, would leave fights between kids to continue. I didn't think there would be so much school.

A fourth respondent. however, thought that the regime was too easy:

I thought it would be much harder than this. It's too easy for half of them — they take advantage. Some staff here are really soft. Kids can swear at staff here and nothing happens.

The typical preconception of what secure accommodation would be like came from one individual who thought:

We'd be locked up in our cells all day, rubbish food and tough staff. I certainly didn't think we'd have school all day, be allowed TVs and stereos in our bedrooms and be able to have outings.

Despite this prevalent fear of being bullied whilst in secure accommodation, only one pupil reported experiencing this problem. He stated that it occurred when he first arrived at the unit and was quickly resolved by a meeting between himself, the bully and a member of staff.

The majority of pupils were also apprehensive of the type of regime that would exist in secure accommodation but all ten interviewees reported that it was not as strict as they thought it would be. Nine of the ten individuals were pleasantly surprised by the regime operating and commented positively on it, but one young man stated it was 'too easy' and perhaps felt the need to be punished by being subjected to a much harsher system. He stated that he would have preferred a stricter regime to have been operating.

3. Views on the appropriateness of secure accommodation

Eight out of the ten interviewees stated that they felt they needed to be in secure accommodation. The two exceptions had similar rationales behind their arguments. One answered, 'because I'm not a threat to the public', whilst the other stated:

> What happened was an accident. It was my first time in trouble. The other lad was drunk. I don't drink. My family would have supported me outside.'

Seven of the remaining eight respondents indicated that their anti-social behaviour would have continued, or even worsened, if they had not been placed in secure accommodation. Comments such as these were prevalent:

> ... the offence was a violent one. I was getting more and more out of control.

> If I hadn't been put away I think I would have got it into my head that I could do that sort of thing and get away with it.

> because it keeps me out of trouble.

One young man even admitted:

> I'm a danger to society that's why I have to see a psychiatrist.

The remaining interviewee said that the principal reason for his incarceration was:

... for my own protection. People are after me where I come from —
because of the nature of the offence.

Surprisingly, eight of the ten pupils said that they needed to be in secure
accommodation. This is consistent with the conventional justifications
found by other researchers such as Cawson and Martell (1979), Harris
and Timms (1993), Hoghughi (1978) and Millham et al (1978), whose
respondents acknowledged that they felt that their freedom would result
in harm to themselves and/or others.

4. Perceptions of punishment

Nine of the ten subjects felt that they needed to be punished for the crimes
they had committed and accepted that the loss of freedom was an appropriate sanction.

> I'm locked up, away from my family, friends and girlfriend. Can't do
> what I like when I like, can't even make myself a cup of coffee when
> I feel like it.

> I'm locked up, have to do as I'm told all the time. I miss the fresh air
> and my home.

The one dissenting voice felt that there was no element of punishment in
this secure unit:

> It's too easy here. Not a punishment, more of a holiday camp.

The interviewees were also asked if they regarded being placed in secure
accommodation as sufficient punishment for what they had done. Eight
out of ten of them felt that it was, though two would have been prepared
to accept even stronger sanctions:

> I think I should have had a fine as well and have a suspended sentence
> hanging over me when I leave here. I need a threat to help me keep
> out of trouble.

> It's too soft here. I should have got twelve months in a YOI (Young
> Offenders' Institution). It's harder there.

In addition to the punitive aspect of placement, the majority recognised
that there were elements of treatment and reform:

I needed to be locked up to teach me a lesson and so I could get some help with my problems, particularly drugs and my temper.

I think I deserved the five years that I got. The judge did me a favour because I could have gone on to kill somebody.

I need say one year in a psychiatric hospital like Broadmoor to help me with my behaviour problems.

If I hadn't been locked up I would have got worse. At least now I'm getting some help.

This recognition that they needed to be both punished and helped is consistent with the writings of Carlebach (1970), Cawson and Martell (1979), Ditchfield and Catan (1992), Harris and Timms (1993). Pupils identified drug abuse counselling, psychiatric care and anger-management courses as treatment areas needed to help them with their problems.

5. Pupils' aspirations

The subjects were asked what they hoped to achieve during their stay in secure accommodation. Their responses again highlighted an expectation that they would receive treatment in addition to being punished by the removal of their liberty. The personal aims they articulated were of three types: behavioural, educational and personal.

Six out of the ten interviewees expressed a need to control their emotions and their behaviour:

I need to learn to control my temper....I must try not to get wound up so easy.

I'm doing an anger-management course with staff. I gotta deal with it now or it will get me into trouble in later life.

I've got to get my behaviour under control. I was out of control before I came here.

All ten subjects had educational aspirations and were involved in external examination work, six having been entered for at least one GCSE examination:

I have to continue with my GCSE work so that when I go back to school I won't be too far behind.

I need to learn to read better because I haven't been to school for years.

Another was keen to pass exams to 'make my mum proud of me for once.'

This interest in educational achievement is again consistent with the findings of other researchers such as Fletcher (1993) who interviewed young people in security. Among the personal objectives held by the pupils were the following:

... this is a chance to come off drugs and stay off.

get psychiatric help ... maybe the psychiatrist can help me.

I need to grow up a bit.

... repair the damage I've done to my family.

It was clear that a priority for the majority of interviewees was to control their tempers. They realised that this had been a problem which had got them into trouble in the past and, if not dealt with, would lead to more serious difficulties in the future.

All pupils hoped to make educational gains. This finding is consistent with the writings of Fletcher (1993) and Garner (1993) who found positive attitudes to learning amongst 'disruptive' students.

6. Educational experience:

The educational experience of pupils involved in serious delinquency has long been recognised as a problematic aspect of their early lives. When asked where they had received their education during the twelve months prior to arrival at the secure unit, it was not entirely surprising that six of the ten had received no formal schooling. Three of the remaining four had attended mainstream schools but had truanted regularly.

A supplementary question concerned truancy rates and the number of school days regularly attended during the past twelve months. All ten respondents stated that their stay in secure accommodation had had educational benefits for them. Six of them felt that they would not have been attending school if they had not been placed in security.

I'd never have been doing GCSEs if I was outside. I wouldn't even have been going to school.

It's been really good for my education. I've not been to school for two years since I got expelled.

I'm learning to read and write and I'm getting good at woodwork and art. I like school. I didn't think I would, but I do.

The pupils were also asked to rate the effectiveness of the teaching at the secure unit. The majority felt that their teachers were very effective. The comments they made about their teachers included the following:

They're good teachers, they'll spend time with you if you don't understand something. It's easier in small groups to get the attention.

They're patient and everything they teach me I'll need in later life.

some are good, some aren't. It's better with small groups. Less hassle. Less arguing.

They try really hard to get you to understand things. You can't skive so easily in here because the groups are so small.

In addition to the positive evaluation of their teaching, the pupils specifically mentioned the benefits of the small educational groups in which they could obtain more teacher help and attention.

Six of the ten pupils admitted that they had been expelled from at least one school during their chequered academic careers and recognised that they would not have been receiving any education if they had not been placed in secure accommodation. High levels of non-attendance were also found in a study of young people in children's homes by Maxwell (1994)

7. Plans for the future

Eight of the ten pupils planned to return home and either get a job, return to school or attend college. The two respondents who did not visualise their futures in this way were serving long sentences and realised that when they left secure accommodation they would have to enter the penal system. One stated:

I'll probably have to finish my sentence in prison

Another felt:

I definitely won't be going home. I'll have to go to prison and I'll probably be there for a very long time.

Seven of the ten interviewees expressed a belief that they would not re-offend when they left security:

> I won't get into trouble again because I don't want to be locked up again and my anger-management course is helping me with my temper.

> I've got a long sentence and by the time I get out I'll have learned my lesson and I'll have grown up quite a bit.

> My family will help me to keep out of trouble. I'll get a job with my mum and I won't need to steal.

The three remaining pupils felt that the outside environment would provide them with too much temptation:

> When I get back with my mates and start taking drugs again, I'll get into trouble again.

> I hope not because I don't want to be locked up again — but I don't know if I'll be able to control myself.

> I'll try not to but when I go home I don't know if I'll be able to resist the temptation. Let's face it, there's not much out there for me, is there?

Experience in the secure unit has enabled most of these young men to develop some optimism about their future. Not only was a deterrent effect acknowledged, but the benefits of treatment and education were recognised. Unfortunately, long-term studies of graduates of secure units would suggest that the more pessimistic prognoses were the more realistic. The study by the Dartington Social Research Unit (1989) shows that the transition to life in the community was seldom smooth. Seventy percent were re-convicted within four years of leaving and the majority remained dependent upon statutory services.

8. Opinions on improving secure units

Four of the ten respondents felt that the secure unit in which they were resident should admit only those detained for long sentences under Section 53 of the Children and Young Persons Act. 1933. They did not think it appropriate that they should have to mix freely with young people on remand or those whose stays were a maximum of three or six months.

They felt that remand or short-stay pupils often received much more staff attention than they did. Young people on remand 'had nothing to lose'. Their poor behaviour resulted in staff having less time to spend with the long-stay residents. They also thought that they received fewer educational and social outings because members of staff were needed to supervise individuals on remand. One young man felt that remand pupils 'mess it up for everyone by mucking about all the time'.

Suggestions for improving the regime of the unit included more time in lessons:

> ... time goes faster when you're at school, it's not so boring. Sundays are boring because there's no school.

A major issue for five of the ten interviewees was the lack of fresh air in the unit. One recommended:

> I would have no bars on the windows so that you could stick your head through and get some fresh air when you really needed it.

Another felt that there should be a set time everyday when every resident could go out of the secure unit on to the secure yard and have ten minutes in the fresh air. He stated that especially in winter, it was possible to have to go for long periods without being out in the fresh air.

A corollary of this last point was the opinion that there should be more educational and social outings taking place. The justification for this was succinctly put by one young man who said:

> How do they know if I'll be all right on the outside if they don't give me a chance to prove it?

Harris and Timms (1993) have referred to the problems of matching provision of secure accommodation to the needs of particular groups of young people and the view of the respondents in the present study about the accommodation of different types of pupils (long-term and remand) are significant. While the long-term residents may suffer some reduction in attention and opportunity, it is also doubtful whether young people on remand who have not yet been found guilty should be associated with those who have been convicted of very serious offences.

Conclusions

Although the numbers of young people detained under Section 53 of the Children and Young Persons' Act 1933 are relatively small, issues relating to the quality and effectiveness of the facilities provided for them are important. These centres are testing grounds for methods of treatment and management and their experience is of potential value to other sectors of the child care system, indeed to the education service in general. In attempting to assess the value of such provision it is essential to heed the views of those for whom it exists. As Vullamy and Webb (1993) say of all children with special educational needs, it is vital that their concerns are adequately described and clearly presented for others to consider.

In the case of the secure unit residents, their experiences, opinions and perceptions provide important feedback on the effectiveness of provision for some of the most socially isolated and disturbed young people. Opportunities for formally stating their views can also provide them with a sense of worth and value, particularly when this contributes to change within the system.

This study provided a number of important insights which have a direct relevance to the development of secure unit provision. First, several respondents mentioned that they had spent a period of time in prison because no secure accommodation places were immediately available for them at the appropriate time. Whilst it is acknowledged that the provision of secure places is extremely expensive, it is imperative that there are enough places available at all times to meet demand. The Home Office currently has plans to create five new secure training centres for two hundred young offenders (White, 1994) but it is equally important that this accommodation is used for the right purpose. The concern about mixing within one facility young people with differing degrees of disturbance and differing needs was raised by the respondents in this study.

Their reflections on the educational benefits provided by the Centre were both heartening and instructive. Despite having experienced seriously disrupted schooling and even ending up deprived of their liberty, these 'problem pupils' continued to harbour educational ambitions and were enhancing their self-esteem through educational achievements. There was also a pervasive feeling that time went faster when 'at school' and that life was not so boring. There is possibly a case for extending the educational programme to include time at the weekends and in the evenings, organised on a modular basis with a requirement to attend a minimum number of sessions but with the option for extra lessons.

The acknowledgement by the majority that they needed to be in secure accommodation and that they deserved to be punished for their wrong-doings was striking. The accompanying recognition that they needed and expected to be helped was also significant and underlined an important principle for the rehabilitation of young offenders expressed as follows by Hoghughi (1978):

> The only way to ensure that he does not return (to society) as an avenger is to have done something with him or for him to make him a happier and better adapted person than the one who went in' (page 241)

References

Carlebach, J. (1970) *Caring for Children in Trouble*, London, Routledge and Kegan Paul

Cawson, P. and Martell, M. (1979) *Children Referred to Closed Units, Department of Health and Social Security Statistics and Research Division, Research Report No. 5.* London, HMSO

Cooper, P. (1992) Exploring Pupils' Perceptions of the Effects of Residential Schooling on Children with Emotional and Behavioural Difficulties, *Therapeutic Care and Education*, 10, 1, 22-34

Dartington Social Research Unit, (1989) *The Experiences and Careers of Young People Leaving Youth Treatment Centres*, Bristol, University of Bristol

Ditchfield, J. and Catan, L. (1992) *Juveniles sentenced for serious offences*, London. Home office

Fletcher, B. (1993) *Not just a Name: The views of young people in foster and residential care*, London. National Consumer Council

Garner, P. (1993) What Disruptive Students Say About the School Curriculum and the Way it is Taught, *Therapeutic Care and Education*, 2.2, 404-415

Hammersley, M. and Atkinson, P. (1983) *Ethnography Principles in Practice*, London Routledge and Kegan Paul

Harris, R. and Timms, N. (1993) *Secure accommodation in Child Care: Between Hospital and Prison or Thereabouts*, London, Routledge and Kegan Paul

Hoghughi, M. (1978) *Troubled and Troublesome: Coping with Severely Disordered Children*, London. Burnett Books

Howe, T. D. (1993) *An Examination of the Perceptions of Pupils with Emotional and Behavioural Difficulties who have Attended a Residential School* Unpublished MEd thesis, University of the West of England, Bristol.

Maxwell, E. (1994) Children in care miss out on school, *Times Educational Supplement*, 10.6.94, p1

Millham, S. Bullock, R. and Hosie, K. (1978) *Locking Up Children: Secure Provision within the Child Care System*, Farnborough, Saxon House.

Vulliamy, G. and Webb, R. (eds) (1992) *Teacher Research and Special Educational Needs*, London, Fulton

White, C. (1994) SSI Inspection uneasy over secure centres, *Care Weekly,* 323,1

150

Chapter 9

Gaining Access to Pupil Perspectives

Robert G. Burgess

The last ten years have witnessed a series of major developments in social and educational research. No longer do we need merely to rely on 'methods' textbooks to gain access to the ways in which such research is conducted, analysed, written and reported. Instead, there is a vast range of specialist materials that take up methodological topics in a series of substantive fields including education. As a result, practitioners as well as researchers are now able to gain access to a range of approaches that can be used when conducting small scale investigations (such as those reported in this volume).

The study of educational settings can cover a range of locations: schools, classrooms, playing fields, workshops, assembly halls, dining halls, changing rooms, cloakrooms, bicycle sheds and so on. In turn, there are also many participants: teachers, pupils, parents, school secretaries, governors, educational administrators, caretakers and many other adults who come onto school sites. Similarly, the study of educational settings can involve a range of topics: nursery classes, science lessons in primary schools, games lessons, cookery classes with children and with adults in further and adult education, as well as all the different subject activities. Yet this is to focus only on the formal aspects of schooling which includes a range of locations and participants. There is therefore, considerable scope for researchers to engage in studies of the educational circumstances that surround the process of schooling. However, we have relatively few studies that go beyond conventional schooling by focusing on patterns of interaction between teachers and pupils. Accordingly, methodological discussions have a tendency to use education as an example of research activity where even those accounts from qualitative researchers provide little detail of the different methodologies required when working in a State or Independent School, nursery class or secondary classroom, academic rather than practical class and so on. Furthermore, in dealing with education and the study of schooling there has been a tendency to overlook the subtleties involved in working with teachers rather than pupils.

Researching Pupil Culture

Much of the work that has been conducted by ethnographers working in schools and classrooms has focused on teacher-pupil interaction. In short, an attempt has been made to understand the culture of schooling from the perspective of the two major parties involved in the school setting. Yet if sociologists and others engaged in school based studies broaden their field of vision, a different picture could emerge.

At the present time, much of our understanding of what goes on in classrooms takes either a teacher perspective (with many ethnographers taking a teacher role) or an adult perspective. Indeed, Peshkin (writing of his experience in a volume with Glesne) notes that although he did not take a teacher role he found himself placed by students in that role, as he reports:

> The class was devoted to students writing paragraphs to go with their thesis paragraph already submitted. The thesis paragraph contained a quote from Huck Finn, a statement given to them about Twain, and their opening statements. The students worked on their own or came to Jane (their teacher) for a reaction to their paragraphs. Then they started coming to me and kept coming for about half the period. They

seemed to have decided that I was functioning as if I were a teacher (Glesne and Peshkin, 1992, p.57).

Automatically, this raised for Peshkin the implications of being incorporated into the teacher role and how this had the potential to conflict with a research role. Indeed, age and status may result in difficulties for researchers who want direct access to the culture of the student body. Even when sitting in classrooms, the age, dress, demeanour and role of the adult, places the researcher in relation to other adults and in relation to pupils.

Many qualitative researchers have set themselves the task of understanding classrooms from a pupil's point of view. This has resulted in some commentators such as McNamara (1980) arguing that there is a danger of researchers taking sides when looking at the school and classroom from the perspective of a pupil rather than a teacher. In particular, McNamara remarked:

In his study of school discipline Woods (1975) clearly indicates where his unexamined sympathy lies and while indicating that the teacher has a problem he fails to appreciate how it may appear to the teacher and how, within the context of an actual lesson, he might resolve it. Woods is concerned with aspects of unofficial punishment in schools: the public showing up of pupils who deviate from the norm. He recognised the importance of this punishment technique during a two-term period of field study in a secondary modern school and his discussion is based upon transcripts of lessons and recorded interviews with pupils. (McNamara 1980, p.119)

However, it is important to recall that this critique of Woods' work is based upon the following interchange:

Christine: I don't like that subject because I can't stand the teacher. I've never really liked him since I got caught skiving, and he made that right fool of me, and I sat next to Kevin ... don't you remember? ... I've never been so bright red in all my life.

Interviewer: What did he say?

Christine: Oh nothing, I'm not telling you.

Interviewer: Come on, tell us what he said.

Christine: I was sitting next to Kevin and he'd got his cartridge
               in his pen and he was going like that (she indicates an
               obscene gesture), and I just pushed him away, and the
               teacher was writing on the board and he must have
               eyes in the back of his head ... and he says ... he turns
               round with a fuming face and he says 'will you two
               stop fiddling with each other!' I never went so bright
               red in all my life, and he pushed me over one side and
               him on the other ... and everybody turned round, didn't
               they ... in front of all my friends! You know ... he made
               such a ... mockery ... can't stand him! Everybody was
               scared stiff in that class, everyone just sits there, all
               quiet. (Woods 1975, pp.134-135)

On the basis of this conversation the following conclusions were made by
Woods:

> This vividly portrays the consumer's experience and a common
> teacher problem. So acutely had she felt the embarrassment that she
> found it very difficult to relate, but having started almost by accident,
> she responded to her three friends present, and addressed most of her
> remarks to them. There was no doubting the intensity of the hostility
> felt towards the teacher in question, chiefly based on that one incident.
> According to Christine's account, she was the victim of both Kevin
> and the teacher. With Kevin, however, it was privatised. The teacher
> made the matter public, implied illicit sexual activity, very plausibly
> to others perhaps because the pair were sitting at the back unseen, and
> everyone discontinued activity to turn around and gaze. This sudden
> transformation of position vis-a-vis others, from being at the back one
> moment, to being at the front the next is a necessary feature of the
> 'Shock' show-up. That her closest friends were present made things
> worse, and that it was a 'mockery' of what had actually been happen-
> ing compounded her sense of injustice. (Woods 1975, pp.134-135)

While Peter Woods was reporting how pupils reacted to being 'shown up'
in the classroom, it was set in a broader context of how pupils respond to
teachers. This account is only part of the story of what occurs in classrooms and a part of teacher-pupil interaction. However, as Delamont
(1992) indicates, the same material could be used by ethnographers in the

1990s studying sexual harassment in schools, given that the 'case' rests upon an example where Kevin makes an obscene gesture across a classroom to Christine. In part, this conjecture by Delamont points to the fact that ethnographers have now sought to gain access to a wider range of pupil experiences including sexuality (Halson, 1992), racism (Troyna and Hatcher, 1992), and child abuse. In dealing with topics associated with pupil experience, researchers working in the field need to understand how sensitive issues can be handled.

Researching Sensitive Issues

A major problem for those engaged in researching sensitive topics is summed up by the question: What counts as a sensitive issue? For some it may appear self explanatory, while for others the term may be used relative to the research context. A situation, circumstance or event that is 'sensitive' for one person may not be so for another. However, Sieber and Stanley (1988) have provided some assistance in this area by defining socially sensitive research as:

> studies in which there are potential consequences or implications, either directly for the participants in the research or for the class of individuals represented by the research.

They continue with two everyday rather than exotic examples drawn from the world of education when they state:

> A study that examines the relative merits of day care for infants against full time care by the mother can have broad social implications and this can be considered socially sensitive. Similarly, studies aimed at examining the relation between gender and mathematical ability also have significant implications.

The result is that researchers need to consider not only how a topic might be considered to be sensitive in terms of data collection procedures, but also how sensitivity may be associated with dissemination and the implications that flow from a research project.

Many of the accounts in this volume bring together the two threads that have been briefly introduced in this chapter. First, examining the educational experience from the pupil perspective. Secondly, examining topics concerned with the pupil experience that are associated with truancy, bullying, aggression, delinquency and an inability to conform to traditional patterns of schooling. It is essential that we acquire an understanding of these aspects of schooling and of pupil experience, but the researcher needs to consider some of the methodological problems associated with such studies and how they might be resolved — a topic that is explored in the remainder of this paper

Taking Sides?

We have already seen that sociologists engaged in qualitative work in schools and classrooms have been accused of taking the 'side' of pupils as against teachers. However, it could be argued that in those cases where sociologists and educationalists have focused on schools and classrooms in order to gain access to social processes associated with teaching and learning, the perspective has been dominated by the teacher point of view and biased in favour of teachers. In these circumstances, the pupil perspective has been lost from view. Certainly, the question of taking sides has been thoroughly examined by Howard Becker and Alvin Gouldner around the question 'Whose side are we on?' The important point is not so much the side that is taken, but the perspective from which work is conducted. Furthermore, it is important that the investigator demonstrates who he or she is working with in order to get accounts from a particular student perspective. Rather than arguing about the taking of sides, it is more important to focus on the different sides that can be taken. Research needs to be open to the possibility of not merely exploring the perspectives of pupils in schools and classrooms, but those of pupils drawn from a variety of backgrounds confronting a range of different circumstances. For example, accounts can be given of the 'best pupil' role. However, we also need accounts of disruptive pupils and the ways they perceive schools and classrooms. Similarly, pupils who are among the alienated, those who are among the repressed, those who espouse lesbian and gay sexualities are suitable for study. All of these groups need to find a voice within the school system. How do they go about finding a voice and presenting themselves within sets of educational circumstances? We know relatively little at the present time beyond what happens in traditional schools and classrooms. Yet once again the assumption is made that all pupils are the same, and all studies can be conducted in similar ways. This raises a number of other ethical issues that we need briefly to explore.

(a) Overt Versus Covert Research

A key argument in the literature on ethics has been concerned with the extent to which research should be overt or covert (Bulmer, 1982). The problem in many educational studies is that research is overt to teachers and other adults, but covert to pupils. In this respect, it is incumbent upon the researcher to explore ways in which the research enterprise can be made more overt, and to detail ways in which the researcher can begin to understand the world of pupils and to make that world publicly accessible to others. In this respect, research conducted in schools and classrooms needs to explore ways in which the central purpose of the research enterprise can be discussed with pupils. How, for example, might we explain a research project to a four year old in a nursery school? How might we gain access to the world of the absentee? How can we conduct studies of bullying from the perspective of the bully? These are all important questions that need to be confronted by social researchers who are grappling with ways in which research should be made more accessible to a wider public (A debate that was clearly signalled by the publication of the White Paper entitled *Realising our Potential*, HMSO, 1993).

(b) Informed Consent

Within numerous ethical codes and statements of ethical principles we find that the doctrine of informed consent takes centre stage. Fundamentally, informed consent refers to ways in which researchers should make sure that all those who engage in research activities are fully informed as to what the research will involve and do so with their consent. Yet again this presupposes that the researcher is in a position to explain in a clear and coherent way the styles and strategies that are to be adopted in the research project. It also presupposes that the explanation is shared between equals. Yet there are problems when an adult works with the under fives, or when male researchers work with teenage girls, or when white researchers investigate racism with black students. The relationships are unequal. When the researcher attempts to explain the content of his or her research to a student group, it challenges them to make clear the kinds of concepts that are important within the social sciences and the ways in which those concepts can be explored so that all parties engaged in the project know the conditions under which they are participating. Yet this presupposes that the researcher knows the direction in which the research will go, and how the research evidence will be used. This is often problematic and needs to be explored with some care. Certainly, individuals have a right to know how researchers are going to work with them, the subject areas that will be covered, and the way evidence will be used. Often, when qualitative studies are returned to individuals, surprise is expressed about the use of quotation and the way in which actual words and phrases are used. In this respect, the investigator needs to explain to all pupils engaged in studies how their words will be utilised in the course of reporting an investigation, but also the circumstances in which the report will be made.

(c) Anonymity and Confidentiality

It is virtually standard practice in studies of a qualitative or ethnographic kind to provide anonymity and confidentiality to all those concerned. This often involves changing the names and locations of the studies, but also modifying the names and circumstances of the individuals that are researched. Reports that are conducted in schools are often returned to institutions, not for the students to check them, but for headteachers (and in some cases teachers) to look at how the study has been reported. Researchers need to be aware of the extent to which pseudonyms that are used with the intention of covering the names of institutions, departments, and individuals may be sufficient to disguise them from the gaze of a wider public, but is not sufficient when being read in the location where the research was conducted. Further steps need to be taken to ensure confidentiality for all concerned. In this respect, when using material drawn from observations, interviews and private diaries, it is important that the researcher does not inadvertently grant access to the world of an individual through not paying sufficient attention to how situations can be disguised.

Many people will argue that the issues and problems that have been raised in this section can be easily covered by using a code of ethics, or a statement of ethical principles. However, these are often framed in very broad terms, with the result that they are designed to provide a framework within which researchers can operate. But more consideration needs to be given to how codes can be established for working with children and with pupils. Thus the rights of the individual are placed alongside the obligations that a researcher has to those who do not have adult status. For example, in what terms might interviews and observations be conducted? What might be the mechanisms associated with reporting research evidence and having that evidence checked out? These are important elements that may be easily covered in a standard agreement, but raise particular questions about the ethical responsibilities of the researcher to children and young people; especially the access which they have to these groups.

Gaining Access

The accessibility of the researcher to the researched is a central issue in all investigations. The key issue is often how access is to be obtained. Indeed, in an earlier review I indicated how access was linked with sponsors, gatekeepers, the members of an institution and those who befriended the researcher (Burgess, 1991). This may be suitable for handling the question of access in the adult world, but it is rare for such groups to involve or include children. Accordingly, we need to think about the way in which access may be granted or withheld in certain settings where children are involved.

Physical access to pupils is often reported to have been obtained through headteachers and teachers, and in some cases through parents. Letters are often written by the researcher to explain the research objectives and how research may involve a combination of observation, interviews and requests to keep research diaries and so on (Burgess, 1994). However, such requests overlook the party to whom access is being requested. How often are pupils given the possibility of participating in research or withholding their agreement to participate? Physical access is often assumed by those who work in social and educational research, so that access to the pupil world is achieved through adults.

But access also has a social dimension. As several investigators have indicated, access is achieved partly through age and through gender. Many years ago, Paul Corrigan (1979) indicated the difficulties of the tall postgraduate researcher in his early 20s working with a group of teenagers. In this respect, it is difficult for researchers to gain complete access to the world of the school pupil given their own personal attributes. Studies that have been conducted in school now range far beyond the formal educational experience. Those studies that concern sexuality and racism cannot presuppose that the gender or ethnicity of the researcher can be taken as read. Special consideration needs to be given to the way in which a combination of personal attributes such as age, gender, ethnicity and social class might influence how the researcher operates. Indeed, the researcher in his or her mid 20s may appear 'young' in relation to teachers, but nevertheless still has adult status. There are relatively few social and educational researchers who have attempted to pass as pupils (Llewyllen, 1980), although even in these circumstances one needs to question whether it is important to actually step into the role of pupil in order to understand that role completely. Does it mean that the work that is done among pupils focuses more heavily on the observer as participant role rather than on the participant as observer role in order to successfully bring off a view of the pupil world?

Strategies and Methods of Social Investigation

The issues that have been raised so far have focused on fundamental questions that have to be asked when working with children and young people and which may well influence the selection of strategies and methods of work.

(a) *Selection*
For any researcher, a series of key questions need to be addressed at the outset of any study. They include:

- Who do I study?
- What do I study?
- When do I study it?

All these matters are concerned with sampling procedures. But in the case of school pupils (especially those who could be described as the disturbed, the alienated, and those who are discriminated against), it is not easy to establish a sample. It is impossible for researchers to go into schools asking bullies to nominate themselves for interview, or for researchers to ask pupils to declare their sexuality prior to the beginning of research. Accordingly, such research needs to be based on the principles of snowball sampling which encourages the researcher to focus on friendship groups. This may have the disadvantage of not being representative of any particular group, but it has the advantage that those students who are seen as being important to one another work alongside the researcher. They may take the researcher into new locations within and beyond the institution. It is they who suggest groups with whom the researcher could work and can discuss the research problem in some detail. In this context, researchers need to consider how some of these pupils may become key informants.

(b) *Key Informants*
The idea of a researcher working with a key informant is well established in the anthropological literature and in those elements of sociology which focus on ethnographic studies. Some examples drawn from the literature are as well known as the studies themselves. Doc, in Whyte's *Street Corner Society*, is a classic example (Whyte, 1955), where Doc took Whyte into a variety of groups and gave him insights into the world which needed to be observed. It is this facility that the adult researcher needs from pupil informants. Accordingly, researchers need to consider how working with key informants may take on a specific perspective which will give insights that are important for their research. However, in working with particular students cast in the role of key informant, it is important to consider the kind of view they represent, the kind of perspective they offer and the access they grant to some situations while automatically blocking access to other groups (Burgess, 1985). The result is that the researcher will need to work with a range of pupil informants in the course of any investigation. These informants may be located in different groups, and may assist the researcher in gaining access to those groups and to particular dimensions of the school setting. Subsequently, this can be linked to the activities that can be observed by the researcher.

(c) *Observation*
We have already noted how the term 'participant observation' might over-state the case of what actually goes on in social and educational research when working with children and young people. Certainly, it would be difficult to deny that participation of some kind occurs at all levels of an investigation. But it is also important to consider on whose terms the participation occurs. In studies with young children, the researcher can become involved in the informal activities that occur on playgrounds, in breaktimes and at lunchtimes (Hanna, 1982), but it is also important to remember that the researcher needs to gain access to the pupil world, and

that any invitation to join groups comes from pupils rather than being requested by adults. This is essential if the pupil perspective is to be observed.

The danger involved in any work where observation and participant observation is concerned with children and young people is that the report that is provided gives an insight into the world of children and young people from an adult's point of view. Instead, it is the task of those who engage in observation to gain access to accounts of that world from the participants' point of view. Accordingly, observation may be used as an umbrella term to discuss the key features of observation and participant observation to include some conversational interviews (McCall and Simmons, 1969). For detailed accounts to be given of the pupil world, it is essential that good rapport, and in particular trust, is established between the researcher and the researched. It is this element that is essential if fieldwork is to meet with success when tapping into accounts of the pupil world.

(d) *Documents of Life*

Many researchers (Plummer, 1983; Burgess, 1984) have indicated the importance of documentary evidence in social research in general and qualitative research in particular. However, while it may be found that institutions contain numerous documents which are available to the social researcher, this is not always the case when dealing with pupils. Certainly the school will have a set of documents on pupils: reports, references, letters, files and so on, but these are all written from the teacher perspective, and all give insight into the world of the pupil from a teacher's point of view. In utilising documentary evidence to gain access to the pupil perspective, it is essential to think of ways in which that evidence can be obtained to highlight the pupil perspective.

Among pupils, a vast array of informal documents are generated. These include: notebooks, letters, notes passed around classrooms, diaries and essays. Overall, a division can be made between ready made documents and commissioned documents (Burgess, 1984). Among the ready made materials are notes that pass between pupils in classes and, depending on the access that is granted by pupils, may result in these being made available to the researcher. However, commissioned documents, such as diaries and essays (Burgess, 1994; Delamont, 1992), can hold the potential of giving access to the pupil world. The documents that are solicited from pupils need to be contextualised so that pupils are told about the kinds of evidence that need to be provided, and the kinds of record that needs to be given. Burgess has drawn attention to the way in which such requests may result in very different kinds of diary entry which then raises comparability issues with regard to data analysis. However, I also highlight how such materials give insights into the pupil world which may be subsequently followed up in observation and interview. Similarly, Delamont has indicated how the short essay written for the researcher may give access to the myths and legends that surround the world of schools and classrooms. Accordingly, researchers working with students might well consider how these approaches to social investigation can be incorporated into the research repertoire.

Future Developments

So far, we have concentrated upon traditional approaches to research when conducting qualitative and ethnographic studies. One element that we need to explore is how technology can be used to gain access to pupil experience. This may mean greater use of photographs, cameras and video equipment. Film and photograph may be readily accessible for use with pupils, and may give insights into their world. It provides a record that the researcher may use with observations that he or she has made, and in that sense can be utilised collaboratively with pupils when working on a research project.

We have already seen how photographs and film can be used with children (Walker, 1985, 1993). However, in these circumstances, it is photographs taken by an adult of pupils working together and pupils working with teachers. If we wish to gain access to the pupil world, we need to consider how pupils themselves perceive that world. What are the observations that they would wish to make? What are the perspectives that they would wish to use? How might these perspectives be incorporated into the research that is conducted by the researcher? The use of camera and cine or video camera may have the advantage of giving power to the pupil, and also may help the researcher to gain access and insight into the pupil world. If pupils are encouraged to take photographs in the school and classroom, topics which they consider of central importance will be recorded. It is these photographs and sections of movie that can be used by the researcher in the course of working on an ethnographic study, as these materials can be used as an additional element of observation — observation through the eyes of the informants. Secondly, the material can be used in interviews to encourage pupils to talk about the perspectives which they reveal. Thirdly, they can provide documentary evidence about the world. The potential is considerable, but further work is required if we are to gain insights into how the qualitative researcher may conduct work with children and young people.

Conclusion

Although pupils may seem to be a captive audience in schools and classrooms, it is still evident that social and educational researchers working with children and young people have failed to give sufficient critical reflection to how they work and have failed to be critical of their world, and of the ways in which researchers may gain access to that world. How might researchers work with children and young people? Here, the emphasis has been placed upon a qualitative approach to research. This stance has been taken as it may help to promote the pupil point of view, but in doing so there is a need to modify researcher strategies and to think critically about the work that is to be conducted. Ethnographic and qualitative approaches may use a set of standard procedures, but these need to be adapted to the group with whom the researcher works. Certainly, those engaged in social and educational research need to explore more fully how their methods may be adopted and adapted when working with children and young people. Indeed, it may be important to see how methods may be adapted when working with particular age groups, and particular interest groups in schools, classrooms and other educational settings.

References

Bulmer, M. (ed) (1982) *Social Research Ethics*, London: Macmillan.

Burgess, R.G. (1984) *In The Field*, London: Allen and Unwin.

Burgess, R.G. (1985) 'In the company of teachers', in R.G. Burgess (ed) *Field Methods in he Study of Education*, Lewes: Falmer Press.

Burgess, R.G. (1991) 'Sponsors, gatekeepers, members and friends: Access in educational settings', in W.B. Shaffir and R.A. Stebbins (eds) *Experiencing Fieldwork*, Beverley Hills: Sage, pp.43-52.

Burgess, R.G. (1994) 'On diaries and diary keeping', in N. Bennett, R. Glatter, and R. Levacic (eds), *Improving Educational Management,* London: Paul Chapman Publishing, pp.300-311.

Corrigan, P. (1979) *Schooling the Smash Street Kids*, London: Macmillan.

Delamont, S. (1992) *Fieldwork in Educational Settings*, Lewes: Falmer Press.

Glesne, C. and Peshkin, A. (1992) *Becoming Qualitative Researchers*, New York: Longman.

Halson, J. (1992) 'Sexual harassment, oppression and resistance: A feminist ethnography of some young people from Henry James School'. Unpublished PhD thesis, University of Warwick.

Hanna, J.L. (1982) 'Public social policy and the children's world: Implications of ethnographic research for desegregated schooling', in G. Spindler (ed) *Doing the Ethnography of Schooling*, New York: Holt, Reinhart and Winston, pp.316-355.

HMSO (1993) *Realising Our Potential*, London: HMSO.

Llewellyn, M. (1980) 'Studying girls at school: The implications of confusion', in R. Deem (ed) *Schooling for Women's Work*, London: Routledge and Kegan Paul.

McNamara, D. (1980) 'The outsider's arrogance', *British Educational Research Journal*, Vol.6, No.2, pp.113-126.

McCall, G.J. and Simmons, J.L. (eds) (1969) *Issues in Participant Observation*, New York: Addison-Wesley.

Plummer, K. (1983) *Documents of Life*, London: Allen and Unwin.

Sieber, J.E. and Stanley, B. (1988) 'Ethical and professional dimensions of socially sensitive research', *American Psychologist,* Vol.43, pp.49-55.

Troyna, B. and Hatcher, R. (1992) *Racism in Children's Lives*, London: Routledge.

Walker, R. (1985) 'Using pictures in a discipline of words', in R.G. Burgess (ed) *Field Methods in the Study of Education*, Lewes: Falmer Press.

Walker, R. (1993) 'Finding a silent voice for the research: Using photographs in evaluation and research', in M. Schratz (ed) *Qualitative Voices*, Lewes: Falmer Press, pp.72-92.

Whyte, W.F. (1955) *Street Corner Society*, Chicago: University of Chicago Press.

Woods, P. (1975) "Showing them up' in secondary school', in G. Chanan and S. Delamont (eds) *Frontiers of Classroom Research*, Windsor: NFER.

Chapter 10

From Data to Action

Richard Davis

The preceding chapters have given insight into the phenomenon of disrupted education. It is a cocktail of issues with different patterns of events but with consistent themes. The children have often had it 'done to them'. It has been less what they brought to the situation than a series of self-fulfilling prophecies. The challenge for us, for we all have an interest as custodians of tomorrow's society, is how to act. What has to be done to stop this evidence from becoming no more than interesting content for more articles and books?

There are ostensibly two foci for action: action to cope with the children who are described in this book and action to prevent such phenomena. The danger is to act without understanding. The field of education is littered with plans implemented with little understanding of the issues, let alone the consequences. To start one needs thorough knowledge and an appropriate perspective. The vital perspective is that of the child and that is why the evidence in this book is so compelling. The focus for action however, lies in the system that has created the phenomena and this is where I want to start. It is also my contention that there is no need to wait for more analysis but that change can take place by 'doing'. Teachers must treat the task as learning by intervention. They are researchers themselves and should be viewed as such.

What I will describe in this chapter is firstly how to understand what it is that needs to be changed and how to think about that change. Secondly, I will show how to use the evidence from studies such as those described in this book to craft action that is likely to lead to sustainable advances. The children are saying 'please listen to us' and though this is common sense, listening to children is not common practice.

I start with a view of the root causes which lie in the system. If it is the system that needs to change then the process for change must be understood. There has been a recent plethora of reports from the likes of Harvard Business Review and Ashridge Management College concluding that most attempts to change organisations fail. This persistent failure has created the myth that change is difficult and takes time. The reality is that change methodology is inept and badly practised. The irony is that the best change thinking originated in education and was pioneered by Bennis, Benne and Chin (1982) in the sixties and seventies and yet has since been largely ignored, not least by the education system.

What the work done in organisations of all descriptions shows, is that there are no palliatives or procedural options. The facts in this book are symptoms of fundamental conditions in the practice of education and it is unlikely that any change will take place by addressing these issues out of context. There are wider factors to be changed first, namely the system-driven behaviours. Although fundamental, it is not inherently difficult to change and good teachers can create astonishing change with understanding and a bit of good leadership.

A perspective on change

There are two primary conditions for change. First, nothing will change unless there is sound understanding of what drives today's behaviour. If change is grafted on without this understanding then it will be undermined by the very things that it is trying to change. Secondly, there is no change unless there is first a change in thinking. These are the two inescapable conclusions of decades of work in organisations.

The work that has led to these conclusions comes from systems thinking. One of the most accessible descriptions of this view is that by Peter Senge (1990) in his book, *The Fifth Discipline*. If change is to be effective and sustainable then organisations need to be viewed as systems. The performance as evidenced in the behaviour of the people and the resulting outcomes is driven by the system.

The evidence in this book is about children who are marginalised and excluded. It is also about frustrated teachers and about considerable waste in time, effort, money and futures of the children involved. There is a strong trend to attribute behaviour to individuals and to look for pathologies in those individuals. Yet Deming (1989) and Juran (1989) and others, who have been the most respected practitioners of organisational effectiveness, have been demonstrating for decades that the way organisations function accounts for most of the variance in performance and the attributes that people bring are largely secondary. In simple terms, it is the context in which people work that makes the difference. If teachers are given clear guidance about what a good job represents, colleagues who help them, feedback about effective action, tools to do the job and managers who pay attention to the right things, then their performance will be much higher than that of those for whom those conditions do not apply. It is the same for the children. If attention is paid to the characteristics of organisation in which they learn and its methods, there is much more scope for improvement than in being concerned with the attributes that they carry.

This does not mean that the notion of individual responsibility is dead. Far from it, it means that individuals who lead a system, in this case, the teachers, have a responsibility to take action on that system and focus improvement on such system conditions. This is no Orwellian view of an all powerful 'system' that denies the individual. It is a view as to how behaviour is formed and an insight into how it can be changed.

The evidence you have read is symptomatic of system conditions. It is crucial to treat it as such because if action is taken on symptoms the result is failure. Furthermore, if these are symptoms then what are the current consequences for the other children who do not become marginalised or labelled? To what extent is their education sub-optimal but simply not conspicuous as such?

If it is upon the system that action must be taken then it must be understood that the system is in turn driven by the way we think and in particular the way its leaders think. This means the leaders at any level, not simply the people at the top. Senge (1990) highlights that not only is waste a symptom of a rotten system but so also are the institutionalised excuses: 'not enough time', 'class sizes' and, in particular, the blaming of outside agencies such as governments. He makes clear the responsibility of the participants by using a quote from a character called Pogo in a Broadway play, 'We have seen the enemy and he is us'.

What this means is that if a school has a low incidence of excluded, marginalised or disaffected pupils then do not collect evidence of what the school is doing differently before collecting evidence of how it thinks. There is encouragement from HMI and other reporting bodies to seek 'best practice' but one of the failures of taking action is that activity is taken out of context, that is, good ideas are replicated but without an understanding of the thinking that underpins them.

Characteristics of the Current System

To the extent that dePear's (1994) study is typical, the primary thinking is predominantly that of command and control. Managers think and teachers do. The tradition is strongly hierarchical with managers treated as more important than teachers. The head teachers are important but importance should be viewed as what they contribute not what they are. Currently, however, it seems that new teachers (NQTs) are treated as the least important members of the system. They are left to fend for themselves in a sort of 'sink or swim' culture. In de Pear's (1994) study a young teacher is quoted as follows: 'Anyone who lacks confidence won't want to admit that they've got a problem'.

If they survive, the view is that they were good people. If they fail, then the view is that they did not have it in them to be good teachers. Nothing could be more redolent of a self-fulfilling prophesy. Yet to a parent or a pupil the most important people are those who spend most time with the children. If the system treats the teachers this way then what is the impact on the pupil?

The most interesting evidence of underlying thinking comes from what managers pay attention to. Ask teachers how they know that they are doing a good job and they are likely to say, 'When no-one pays attention to me', 'When my class is under control', 'When I do not get complaints', etc. There is a culture of what Seddon (1992) calls 'attention to output'. In other words managers manage by the numbers and unless these numbers start to look bad or a complaint hits their desk they leave well alone. The current pressure from government has exacerbated the 'numbers game' with league tables and the current need to attract pupils. This now means that teachers are urged to make the accountable numbers look good. In cultures such as this, people do whatever they need to keep the manager in his or her office. This has not been caused by the government pressure for accountability, it is what the prevailing thinking has *made* of that pressure. It was a problem waiting to happen and is symptomatic of a system that was not paying attention to the right things in the first place. De Pear quotes a competent and well respected teacher who ascribes the school's problems to a lack of control and discipline. Another teacher records, 'The head ticked us off last week at briefing for not controlling the kids'. This exemplifies how deep rooted the thinking is.

Teachers are servants of the hierarchy. The hierarchy manages by procedures in much the same way that the education system manages the schools. This is reflected in the responses of teachers interviewed by de Pear:

> The emphasis is on whether deadlines are being kept not on what is going on in the classroom,
>
> We are forever under pressure to deliver reports
>
> As long as we've got a policy somewhere, we're doing our job.

A further characteristic of the current thinking is that it assumes that it is teachers who must be measured whereas it is the processes and methods that must be measured. Again the government has not helped by stressing the accountability of individuals and by stressing appraisal and perfor-mance related pay. But this is the existing system is exemplified above by the treatment of new teachers, and it dislikes government ideas for different reasons.

The systems perspective encourages a view that there are not good and bad teachers, there is a system that encourages them to think the wrong way and do the wrong things. This is good news because it is much easier to change the way we think than it is to change the way we are. This is the message. Teachers must act on the system that they prop up and not on individuals.

A key theme and implication from this book is the issue of advocacy. What does the current thinking make of advocacy? If the underlying goal is control, then there is no inherent will to listen. Advocacy is treated as a necessary evil: 'We will talk to the children when we need to'. Education tends still to be something that is 'done to' children as opposed to something in which they are engaged. Advocacy is not relevant to thinking such as this. Evidence of the confusion that surrounds this issue is seen in the comparison between the 1989 Children Act where advocacy is a right for the child and in the 1994 SEN Code of Practice where it is merely discretionary.

The emphasis on control is what causes children with difficulties to become 'problem' pupils. Children are ignored because they do not conform to requirements of what is being 'done to' them. For some, the only way that they can elicit attention is by being disruptive. They are then labelled and once labelled there is a strong tendency for the system to engage the procedure of eliminating them.

The outcomes of a system that thinks this way are clear. Teachers waste time coping with disruptive behaviour (Wheldall, Houghton and Merrett 1989). There is the huge cost of dedicated teachers and schools allocated to handling disruptive children. The pupils themselves say that the schools 'won't let us be educated', 'They just didn't want me' (de Pear 1994). Truanting children say that they would rather be in school. This must be viewed as nothing less than colossal waste that has been institutionalised. The latest set of discussion papers from DfE is even titled 'Pupils with Problems' (Circular 8/94). It would appear, therefore, that while teachers claim that they do not have time to put it right, even if they recognise the problem, they have plenty of time to get it wrong.

A method for change

Chin and Benne (1967) have shown that there are only three methods for change: coercion, education and involvement. Coercion is often used in the guise of legislation. It creates change but more in the way of compliance than commitment. Educating people as a change method follows the view of 'do this because you know it is good for you'. This is ineffective as it merely preaches to the converted and pays no attention to what stops people doing it. The typical way in which the 'education' method takes place is for academics to carry out studies which then become enshrined in recommended practice. There is nothing wrong with the studies but with the use to which they are put. Guidelines and procedures are then promulgated from the top but these have no validity as change mechanisms. In fact, they merely enhance the waste in the system by taking up time. They are no more valid than anyone else's opinion in reality. It is no wonder that little change takes place. Yet as Chin and Benne suggest these two 'methods' account for the majority of attempts to change practice.

Teachers do what they do because it makes sense to them in the current regime. They will not change until they see an alternative that makes equally good sense. The only way to create change is to provide them with *data* about the consequences of their action such that *they* can see what it is that they are creating directly and how *their* thinking drives performance. If we give teachers the task of collecting the type of data contained in this book they are more likely to see a need for change. This is not entirely new. Leadbetter and Tee (1991) helped teachers collect such material and showed how it can be used to drive action. The task for educators is then to re-educate teachers using their own data. They will need a systems perspective as outlined above but the data provide the teacher with *informed* choice i.e. if our pupils have these difficulties because of the way we behave and think, then there must be a better set of outcomes. What would we want instead?

The data also provide the knowledge of how to do it. If the data are specified around 'what pupils see us *doing*' then teachers can see what to *do* more of or less of. The primary task is to deal with the conditions that stop teachers treating the problem differently. The conditions will be about thinking, for example, because if managers treat teachers as people to provide information for reports then the real work that they do is not valued. It will prove futile to work on the teacher-pupil relationship without understanding the manager-teacher relationship.

The importance of this view is that the data have validity — they describe the needs from the children's perspective and show what it is that teachers need to act upon in their own situation. It also shows that what they do is driven by how they think and allows substantive change to take place. The data allow teachers to own their own behaviour and stop attributing it to other causes. While it is plausible to state that the institutional view of managing by policy and procedures is unhelpful, wasteful and distracting, it cannot be emphasised enough that the teachers themselves create most of the waste by not owning what they create. They should not be blamed for this, but there is now an opportunity for them to learn — and from themselves.

There is also an opportunity to learn from variance in practice. Instead of generalised opinion coming from the centre, schools all over the country can start to act and learn from their own data. The result is a mass of learning and such collective learning will be more powerful and valid. Change will come from sharing and disseminating empirical work rather than from external academic study and government *fiat*. Variance must be seen as valuable, not as a problem. This is the 'normative' approach of Chin and Benne where the teachers themselves are fully involved in research and change.

How might that look in practice?

The primary requirement is leadership. The first element of that leadership is for managers to be clear about the goal of the system. The principal goal is to engage the pupils in education and provide them with choices for life as the outcome. **Step one** is for the heads to spend time with the teachers clarifying the goal and discussing how different that is from today's practice.

Step two is then to collect evidence that tells them how well the way they work currently delivers against that goal. Where is the evidence? The primary source is the children themselves. They are currently treated as though they do not have the capability to contribute to the debate. It has been shown by contributors to this book that they *do* have a view, if only we asked them (see also Davie 1993). A useful parallel in medicine is the debate about self-administered pain treatment for post-operative patients. Doctors have found that patients are quite capable of assessing their needs and deciding their own doses, hospitals are saving money because the patients use less not more. (The traditional approach is an example of how 'thinking' can create waste.) The message is clear — if pupils are treated as though they are capable of contributing then they can. However, it is salutary to note that sometimes *teachers* are not treated as though they can contribute, let alone the pupils. The current practice in many schools is that managers know best and that the teachers' work schedules have to be dictated.

In parallel with these first steps it is important to start informing and involving the parents. They will have views about the goals and current practice. They also will take their share of implementing the outcomes. Even the local press can be valuable allies, creating recognition of needs and of successes.

Teachers can start to ask pupils what it is that teachers do that allows them, the pupils, to be more engaged and to learn more capably. In the first instance it is possible that pupils will have a largely unsophisticated view of how to respond because they have not been hitherto treated as capable of contribution to issues such as curriculum delivery. The skill of the teacher is to ask questions about those aspects that *do* matter to the pupils and upon which they *will* have a view. The pupils' responses will be used as a means of understanding the way in which the current system operates. At this stage the data is qualitative. This will have more purchase if it is converted into quantitative data: 'where and by how much is this true?' The outcomes of interviews, questionnaires, conversations and observations are translated into a set of statements such as:

- teachers listen to pupils who express difficulty
- teachers encourage pupils to express difficulty
- teachers go out of their way to make lessons interesting
- teachers demonstrate that they understand the needs of pupils
- teachers are seen to be fair in their dealings with pupils
- teachers are seen to be approachable

We have found from experience that people are more comfortable rating positive items. Negative items are seen as 'leading' and the implicit criticism is resented.

Step three is to ask the pupils to rate teachers as a group and/or individually against these items, identifying the extent to which they agree or disagree that it is currently true for them. The resulting data can become the meat for change, describing exactly what needs action (for example, a certain percentage of pupils feel that we do not pay attention to their needs, etc.) **Step four** is for the teachers to discuss the data. This process may highlight facets of general practice or individual characteristics. Some teachers, for instance, may be highly rated on creating interest, encouraging responsibility and responding to pupils' problems. The challenge is to find out exactly what those teachers do and to encourage learning by their colleagues. If the response should be to say, 'Ah but, they are just good teachers', then the point has been missed. The point is that they are good teachers because of what they *do*, not what they *are*. It is likely that all members of staff have something to contribute and something to learn.

The mistake at this stage is to assume that the teachers have the answers, so **Step five** is for the teachers to go back to the pupils with the evidence and engage them in discussion about what it means and how the teachers can start to act. The question to ask of the pupils is, 'If this is what the data says and this is where we need to be, how can we best make this work?'

Step six is to turn this learning into the way the school works from then on. This is a leadership activity. Ideally senior teachers and heads need to spend time in classrooms encouraging teachers to learn from each other and assess the learning that takes place. The questions they should pose are 'Why do the pupils in this class seem to work this way and what is it that the teacher does to encourage it?', 'Who else could learn from this?', 'How can we create a process that encourages that learning?' This is not a one-off activity, it *is the work*. Managers cannot create value unless they work this way. Their purpose in life is to enhance the capability of the process not to control it. This is now a much more competent basis for appraisal where the managers are acting on data from the system, namely, the pupils' view of how effective the learning process is, rather than the managers' opinions of competence. By adopting this approach the senior teacher has data from the pupils and from the teachers' peers that describe the effectiveness of the work they do.

It is likely that many would respond to such a proposal with the question: 'how can we trust the pupils to be honest?' Such a response could be seen as indicative of a system which produces pupil disaffection and problem behaviour. The question to anyone who raises that objection is, 'Who will benefit?' Many teachers have found that once the pupils understand the purpose of the exercise they contribute fully. When they see that the teachers take action on the data they begin to understand the issues even more clearly and will contribute to the more refined issues. It is an iterative process. The likely outcome is that through consultation they come to understand what matters and develop skills that enable them to become more discriminating in their contribution to the process.

This approach is challenging to teachers. In the current climate they may be very uncertain about the use to which the data about them is to be put. This too is a leadership issue. It is the role of the leader to stress that the issue is the system competence and that all teachers can contribute to improvement. The leaders must also act on what is obstructing the improvement, for example, inadequate or inappropriate procedures; fire fighting rather than problem solving; demands for reports etc. If there are statutory requirements that cannot be avoided, accommodating them becomes a joint problem: 'How can we best handle this?'.

It may be that as a result there is the odd teacher who cannot learn or does not want to change. In practice this is much less likely than may be imagined but if so, there is enough evidence for it to be obvious that they must move on. This is a clear principle at work in many organisations and managers discover that the staff who they believed were troublesome were nothing of the sort. Is it not true that people come to work to do a good job? It is primarily how systems have defined jobs that is dysfunctional. If there is data that the teachers have been involved in collecting then the outcomes of that 'research' will be theirs and they will see that the alternative makes sense.

The ongoing role of the leader is to test how well his or her particular 'system' is meeting the goal. Again, the leader will not discover that in the office looking at exam results but only out in the classroom watching and talking to the people who receive and deliver the work. This has significant implications for measurement. Instead of league tables driving behaviour (for example, pupils with special needs being disapplied to minimise the impact on the exam results) there is now measurement of what matters — the learning process in the classroom. The 'leader' has to ask the question, 'Is this measurement continuing to tell us what matters and if so how do we improve it?'

The problem, as ever, is that this process will seem like more work. Despite the fact that there is so much waste in the system, that is only evident after it has been reduced. A helpful step is to create focus for the teachers. This can be done by consensus, that is, agreeing from the data those few items that seem to make the biggest difference. There is a more valid alternative called factor analysis. This is readily available in modern statistical software and analyses the variance in the data to show the core of items that most inform the overall picture. This would provide empirical validity to allow teachers to focus on the 'vital few'. This also allows the leaders to focus on 'How do we know it is improving?' These vital few become the immediate target for re-measurement and the learning process continues. 'Where has it improved? What did we do there? Why did it work and how can we spread the learning?'

The irony is that the output measures such as league tables will improve dramatically anyway if for no other reason initially than by removing the dysfunctional behaviour that surrounds them. This would also appear to be a very effective definition of 'value added'.

The pupils will become used to having responsibility for shaping their own learning. This is not the 'pupil-centred learning' debate. This is a practical focused activity that engages pupils in taking a view about what matters to them. The goals are made clear and the question for them is, 'How can we make this work more effectively?' As Kohn (1993) has highlighted, it is extraordinary that pupils are expected to come out of education with moral courage and responsibility for self and yet they have been given so little while they are *in* the process. This appears to be true for all pupils yet it is especially true of the pupils featured in this book.

There has been significant success in inviting pupils to take responsibility for what happens to others in the 'bullying' context. They can, therefore, show an equal responsibility for handling those pupils who exhibit other kinds of 'problem' behaviour. Over time they can be asked how to structure teaching and learning to take account of those who need more help and those who need more stretching.

In summary, the view taken here is that the system, as driven by the current thinking, contributes significantly to the problems which this book has explored. If there is any likelihood of change it can only come from a sound understanding of how the system drives behaviour. It is the teachers themselves who can create change by collecting and acting on the evidence that tells them how *their* system drives their behaviour. There is much good work that can be done by finding good practice but only in so far as the good practice is understood to be a function of different *thinking* not merely different actions. The Code of Practice (DfE 1994) states, 'The effectiveness of any assessment and intervention will be influenced by the involvement and interest of the children or young people concerned.' (p.14). The Code encourages schools to, 'make every effort to identify the ascertainable views and wishes of the child or young person about his or her current and future education.' (p.14). I look forward to the time when this is reality for all children and not simply a requirement for those with special needs.

References

Bennis, W.G., Benne, K.D., and Chin, R (eds) (1969) *The Planning of Change* New York, Holt, Rinehart and Winston

Davie, R. (1993) *Listen to the Child*, The Psychologist June 1993

Deming, W. Edwards (1989) *Out of the Crisis*, MIT, Centre for Advanced Engineering Study, Cambridge, Mass

Department for Education (1994) *Pupils With Problems C 8/94*. London: DfE

Department for Education (1993) *The 1993 Education Act*. London: HMSO

Department for Education (1994) *The Code of Practice on the Identification and Assessment of Special Educational Needs*. London: DfE

Department of Education and Science (1981) *The 1981 Education Act*. London: HMSO

de Pear, S. (1994) *The Link Between Special Needs and Exclusions. Why?* Unpublished M.Ed. thesis: Brunel University

Juran, J.M. (1989) *Juran on Leadership for Quality: an Executive Handbook* New York: The Free Press (Macmillan Inc)

Kohn, A. (1993) *Punished by Rewards*. Boston: Houghton Mifflin

Leadbetter, J. and Tee, G. (1991) A Consultancy Approach to Behaviour Problems in School. *Educational Psychology in Practice*, 6, 4, 203-209

Seddon, J. (1992) *I Want You to Cheat*. Buckingham: Vanguard Press

Senge, P. (1990) *The Fifth Discipline*. London: Century Business

Wheldall, K., Houghton, S. and Merrett, F. (1989) Natural Rates of Teacher Approval and Disapproval in British Secondary School Classrooms. *British Journal of Educational Psychology*, 59, 38-48

Notes on the Contributors

Judith Anstiss is Co-ordinator of Support Services at Foxford School, Coventry.

Robert Burgess is Professor of Sociology and Director of the Centre for Educational Development, Appraisal and Research at the University of Warwick.

Paul Cooper is a lecturer in emotional and behavioural difficulties at the Cambridge University Institute of Education.

Philip Craig is a teacher at a Social Services secure unit.

Jo Crozier is a part-time lecturer in Education at the University of Warwick Institute of Education.

John Dwyfor Davies is Director of Studies (INSET) in the Faculty of Education at the University of the West of England, Bristol.

Richard Davis is an occupational psychologist with Vanguard Consulting, Buckingham.

Susan de Pear is Special Needs Co-ordinator at a north west Surrey comprhensive school.

Phil Garner is a lecturer in special educational needs at the School of Education, Brunel University.

Tanya Howe is a teacher at a residential special school for children with emotional and behavioural difficulties.

Mel Lloyd-Smith is Deputy Director of the University of Warwick Institute of Education.

Ann Sinclair Taylor is a lecturer in Education at the University of Warwick Institute of Education.

Index of Subjects

academic performance 36, 50, 72, 73, 80, 82, 97, 98, 118, 142- 144, 147
attention-seeking behaviour 53, 55, 56, 61, 63

bullying 36, 42, 57, 116, 138, 157
behaviour management 2, 18, 74

Code of Practice 8, 11, 64, 71,178-179
curriculum 21, 22-24, 28, 45, 64, 68, 73, 119, 121-122

disruptive behaviour
 and girls 38, 39
 forms of 32, 36, 73
 sanctions 35
 teachers' responses 40
disruptive pupils 17-29
 characteristics 36, 73
 segregation of 1, 2, 4, 19
 and the curriculum 22

education market 6, 8
educational psychologists 34, 35
Elton Report 8, 10, 19, 32, 45

emotional and behavioural
 difficulties 2, 73, 74, 87-89, 91, 100, 105, 126
 prevalence 4, 31, 32
 provision 89, 111-131
 exclusion 1, 3, 6, 8, 31, 49-50, 58, 60

family background 64, 112-114,
family discord 36, 44, 55, 56, 63-64, 101, 103, 112

girls and disruption 31-46

identification 32, 35, 50, 51
institutionalisation 63, 90-92, 101, 124-126
integration 2, 4, 18, 29, 68-69, 74, 78-81, 84, 88-89, 126
interpersonal needs 50-53, 114-115
isolation 27, 55, 125-126, 130

labelling 50, 52, 63, 72, 75- 76, 79, 104, 124, 125
legislation:
 Children Act 1989 5, 8, 10, 11, 71
 Children and Young Persons' Act 1933 133

Circular 1/83 10
Circular 9/94 32
Education Act 1981 2, 10, 18
Education Act 1986 3
Education Act 1988 6
Education Act 1993 3, 8, 18, 71
Public Law 94-142 (USA) 18
listening to pupils 8-10, 11, 17, 21,
   70-71
local management of schools 6, 7, 8

marginalisation 6, 34, 45, 76, 79, 83

organisational factors 168-172
organisational change 172-179

powerlessness 50, 103
pupil advocacy 50, 64, 69, 70-72,
   111, 117, 123, 156, 168, 171-
   172, 175
pupil strategies 42, 43, 46
pupils' perceptions 8-11, 70
   girls' perspectives 37-46
   of school 26, 44, 81, 97-99
   of secure provision 136-141
   of teachers 59, 60, 62, 76-78, 99
   of units 74

research methods:
   access 21, 34, 70, 88, 159-160
   documentary evidence 62-63, 70,
      93
   ethical issues 69, 130, 134,
      157-159
   ethnography 91, 152, 155
   grounded theory 91-92
   interviews 20, 37, 50, 51, 70,
      93-95, 112, 134
   observation 32, 50, 70, 93, 95,
      161-162
   qualitative research 153, 156
   questionnaires 93, 112

reflexivity 93-94, 134
selection 160-161
technology 163-164
researching pupil perceptions 11,
   93-94, 151-163
residential provision 89-91, 111,
   133-134
   effects of 97-105, 112-114,
      130-131

school ethos 26, 27, 34, 115
school organisation 17, 26-28, 79,
   98, 106, 115, 118, 125, 140
school rules 11, 18, 23, 26, 27, 28,
   32
secure accommodation 4, 5, 12,
   133-148
self-esteem 51, 62, 75, 79, 103, 115,
   117, 121, 130, 147
social skills 80, 97, 100
special schools 3, 10, 12, 50, 54, 57,
   88-107
special units 18, 67-84
stigma 79, 81, 124
support services 34, 35, 70, 117
systems analysis 168-172

teacher attributes 23-25, 28, 60, 62,
   90, 170-171
teacher expectations 28, 33, 34, 35,
   40, 63, 74, 83, 152
teacher-pupil relationships 99,
   102-106, 117-118, 137, 144, 152-
   155, 175
teaching styles 24, 25, 60, 62, 73,
   118, 144
truancy 36, 42, 43, 144, 172

Wagner Report 88, 90
Warnock Report 68
withdrawal 52, 72

Index of Names

A

Alder, C., 32, 33, 46
Anstiss, J., 12, 31
Atkinson, P., 93, 108, 134, 148
Aubrook, L., 72, 85
Austin, G., 17, 29

B

Balbernie, R., 90, 107
Ball, S., 14, 21, 29, 69, 84
Barton, L., 4 13, 19, 29
Bash, L., 19, 29
Becker, H., 75, 84, 156
Bell, J., 69, 84
Bennathan, M., 4, 13
Benne, K. D., 168, 172, 173, 174, 179
Bennis, W. G., 168, 179
Berridge, D., 4, 13, 89, 108, 127, 131
Bettelheim, B., 90, 107
Bloom, L., 71, 84
Blyth E., 1, 13
Bond, J., 31, 46
Booth, T., 6, 13
Bowe, R., 14
Bridgeland, M., 90, 107
Brown, S., 14

Bullock, R., 89, 108, 149
Bulmer, M., 69, 84, 157, 165
Burgess, R. G., 12, 75, 84, 159, 161, 162, 163, 165
Burn, M., 107

C

Carlebach, J., 142, 148
Carrier, J., 18, 29
Catan, L.,134, 142, 148
Cawson, P., 5, 13 134, 141, 142, 148
Cherrett, P., 89, 108
Chin, R., 168, 172, 173, 174, 179
Clark, M., 18, 29
Cohen, R., 6, 13
Cole, T., 4, 10, 13, 89, 107, 123, 129, 131
Cooper, P. W., 11, 12, 13, 17, 29, 64, 65, 134, 87, 89, 105, 107, 108, 114, 121, 125, 131, 148
Cooper and Lybrand, 7, 13
Corrigan, P., 75, 79, 84, 159, 165
Coulby, D., 13, 19, 29
Craig, P., 4, 12, 13
Cronk, 92, 108
Crozier, J., 12, 31

D
Davie, R., 8, 13, 174, 179
Davies, J., 69, 84
Davies, J. D., 1,
Davies, L., 45, 46
Davis, A., 90, 108
Davis, R., 12, 167
Dawson, R., 9, 15, 89, 90, 108
de Pear, S., 12, 49, 170, 171, 172, 179
Delamont, S., 154, 163, 165
Deming, W. E.,169, 179
Denscombe, M., 72, 85
Ditchfield, J., 134, 142, 148
Docking, J., 18, 29
Dubberley, W. S., 39, 47
Dunlop, A.,103, 108

E
Ecob, R., 108
Elliott, J., 84, 85
Evans, J., 8, 14
Evans, M.,114, 121,
Evans, R., 18, 29

F
Farrington, D.,103, 109
Fernandez, C., 9, 14, 123, 131
Fletcher, B., 143, 148
Flude, M., 15
Fry, L., 14, 15

G
Gallie, W. B., 68, 85
Galloway, D., 124, 131
Garner, P., 10, 11, 14, 17, 29, 143, 148
Gersch, I., 9, 14, 15
Gerwitz, S., 6, 7, 14
Gillborn, D., 17, 29
Giller, H., 103, 109
Glaser, B., 90, 108
Glesne, C., 152, 153, 165
Goacher, B., 4, 14,

Goffman, E.,101, 108
Goodwin, C., 124, 131
Gouldner, A., 156
Green, F., 9, 14
Grimshaw, P., 89, 108
Grimshaw, R., 127. 131

H
Halson, J., 155, 165
Hammer, M., 15
Hammersley, M., 69, 85, 93, 108, 134, 148
Hanna, J. L., 162, 165
Hargreaves, D., 60, 62, 65, 72, 75, 79, 85, 104, 108
Harre, R., 92, 93, 109
Harris, R., 5, 14 133, 138, 141, 142, 146, 148
Hart, S., 20, 30, 69
Hatcher, R., 155, 165
Hester, S. K., 60., 62, 65, 108
Hoghughi, M., 5, 14, 103, 108 141, 148, 149
Holt, J., 63, 65
Hosie, K., 89, 108, 149
Houghton, S., 172, 179
Howe, T. D., 4, 12, 14, 111, 134, 149
Hughes, M., 6, 13
Hurford, 69, 85

J
Jarvie, L., 21, 29
Jones, C., 19, 29
Juran, J. M., 169, 179

K
Kelly, B., 11, 14
Keys, W., 9, 14, 123, 131
Kohn, A., 178, 179
Kyriacou, C., 81, 85

L

Lacey, C., 79, 85
Lahey, M., 71, 84
Lane, D., 9, 14,
Laslett, R., 118, 124, 131
Leadbetter, J., 173, 179
Lees, S., 32, 33, 36, 42, 43, 46
Lennhoff, F., 90
Lewis, A., 11, 14
Llewyllen, M., 160, 165
Lloyd, G.,46, 47
Lloyd-Smith, M., 1, 14, 18, 29, 63, 65
Lovey, J., 18, 29
Lowden, 69, 85
Lunt, I., 8, 14
Lyward, G., 90

M

Macbeth, J., 9, 14
MacNamara, D., 153, 165
Maget, H., 10, 14,
Major, J., 6
Martell, M., 5, 13, 134, 141, 142, 148
Matza, D., 104, 108
Maughan, B., 109
Maxwell, E., 144, 149
Maylis A. S., 15
McCall, G. J., 162, 165
McCann, P., 18, 30
Measor, L., 32, 33, 36, 47
Meier, C.,19, 30
Mellor, F. J. 60, 62, 65, 108
Merrett, F., 172, 179
Millham, S., 5, 14, 89, 108, 141, 149
Milner, J., 1, 13
Minkes, J., 71, 85
Mongon, D., 20, 30
Moon, B., 15,
Moore, M., 9, 10, 11, 15, 68, 71
Mortimore, P., 90, 108, 109
Murtaugh, M., 17, 30

N

Nash, R., 63, 65
Neill, A. S., 90, 108
Nixon, J., 17, 29
Norwich, B., 6, 14

O

O'Keefe, D., 43, 47
Ouston, J., 109

P

Parten, M. B., 79
Pearson, G., 19, 30
Peshkin, A., 152, 153, 165
Pimenoff, S., 9, 14
Plummer, K., 162, 165
Pollard, A., 70, 85
Potter, P., 90, 108
Powney, J., 95, 108
Pringle, M.,103, 108,
Purkey, S., 90, 108

R

Rees, T., 69, 85
Reynolds, D., 17, 29, 90, 108
Riddell, S., 14
Rogers, C.,95, 109
Rosser, E.,92, 93, 109
Ruddock, J., 17, 29
Russell, P., 7, 15
Rutter, M., 90, 103, 109

S

Sacken, D., 20, 30
Sammons, L., 89, 108,
Saunders, S., 3, 15
Sayer, J., 81, 85
Scherer M., 4, 14, 15
Schostak, J., 18, 30, 92, 109
Schutz, W. C., 50, 65
Seddon, J., 170, 179
Senge, P., 169, 170, 179
Sharpe, S., 42, 47
Shaw, O.,90, 109

Sieber, J. E., 155, 165
Sikes, P., 32, 33, 36, 47
Simmons, J. L., 162, 165
Sinclair, R., 71, 85
Sinclair Taylor, A,12, 67
Smith, C., 89
Smith M., 90
Smith, P., 42, 47
Stanley, B., 155, 165
Stanley, J., 38, 47
Stanworth, M., 45, 47
Stevenson, D., 17, 30
Stirling, M., 3, 6, 15
Stoll, P., 43, 47, 108
Strauss, A., 91, 108
Sullivan M., 109
Swann W., 2, 4, 15

T
Tann, 70, 85
Tattum, D., 63, 65, 92, 93, 103, 109
Tee, G., 173, 179,
Thomas, B., 9, 14
Timms, N., 5, 14 134, 138, 141,
    142, 146, 148
Tisdall, G., 9, 15
Tomlinson, S., 4, 13, 19, 29
Topping, K., 124, 131
Troyna, B., 82, 86, 155, 165

U
Upton, G., 64, 65, 89

V
van Niekerk, L., 19, 30
Vulliamy, G., 147, 149

W
Wade, M., 9, 10, 11, 15, 68, 71, 85
Walker, R., 163, 165
Watts, M., 95
Webb, R.,147, 149
Wedell, K., 4, 15
West, A., 69, 84, 103, 109
Wheldall, K., 172, 179
White, C.,147, 149
Whyte, W. F., 161, 165
Willis, P., 92, 109
Wills, W. D., 90, 109
Wilson, M., 114, 121
Wittrock, M., 92, 109
Woods, P., 32, 41, 47, 92, 109, 153,
    154, 165

Z
Zeitlin, A., 17, 30